I0457158

MOON TIME PLANNER

LUNAR-GUIDED 6-MONTH CALENDAR + JOURNAL

JANUARY - JUNE 2023

property of:

_____

_____

_____

_____

Artwork created in collaboration with author and artificial intelligence.
2023 Moon Time Planner, Lunar-Guided 6-Month Calendar + Journal, January - June
Michele Morrow. Paperback ISBN: 979-8-9860099-4-0

INDEX

LIVING ON MOON TIME

It's only natural to keep beat with the Moon - humanity has been doing it forever.

In the beginning it was a matter of survival. Prehistoric people etched animals and Moon Phases onto cave walls, likely tracking and planning Moonlit hunts. When civilization began, Babylonian astronomers used the Moon's annual Lunations to systemize the 1st known calendar, which eventually evolved into the calendar we use today.

1 Lunation = the 29.5 day orbit of the Moon around Earth, aka "Lunar Month". The word "month" actually stems from the word "Moon", sharing the same root and related meaning.

In addition to serving as a natural timekeeper, the Moon is also gravitationally locked with us in a celestial partnership known as "Tidal Force", which causes the daily rise and fall of Earth's oceanic tides.

Farmers have claimed Tidal Force also impacts moisture levels in soil, therefore contributing to the success or failure of their crops. Known as "Astrological Agriculture", practitioners believe that planting specific seeds during optimal Moon Phases can maximize their potential for bountiful harvests.

It's even believed, by some, that the Moon influences human behavior - after all, we are made of nearly 60% water. It begs the question: If the Moon affects our tides and soils, does she affect us, too? *What if we tended to ourselves with Moon Phases in mind?*

The purpose of Moon Time Planner is to encourage intention setting + follow-through by using the Lunar Cycle as a guide. Each month features the 8 Primary Moon Phases with a revolving set of 8 Actions to inspire progress on goals:

1. Manifest | New Moon
2. Progress | Crescent Moon
3. Motivate | 1st Quarter Moon
4. Expand | Gibbous Moon
5. Enjoy | Full Moon
6. Reflect | Disseminating Moon
7. Release | Last Quarter Moon
8. Restore | Balsamic Moon

The daily calendar pages contain journal prompts specifically designed for each day's Moon + Action. Additional features include Astrological forecasts + worksheets every ~2 weeks on New Moons + Full Moons, plus guided, quarterly check-ins based on the 12 Astrological Houses. Keep track of planetary transits + aspects, as well as appointments, intentions, habits, tasks, moods + gratitude.

In the pages that follow, you'll be encouraged to live in sync with something ancient, something vital and something deeply reliable – not to mention, something personal; who hasn't gazed at the Moon lost in thought or amazed by the cosmos? She constantly appears in our art, our conversations and the lyrics to our favorite songs. The Moon is always here for us – ready to provide guidance on how to proceed + connect with our true selves.

HOW MOON PHASES WORK

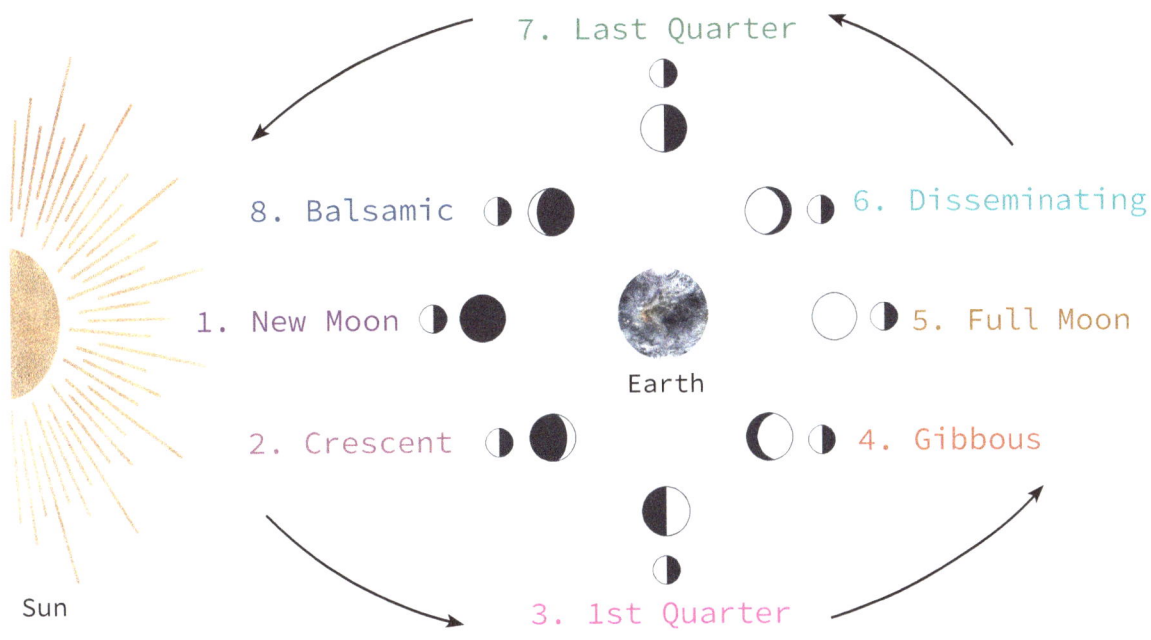

Moon Phases are determined by how much Sun appears to illuminate the Moon's surface as she orbits counterclockwise around Earth. In the chart above, the smaller Moons represent how she appears lit from the view of the Sun, while the larger Moons represent how she appears lit to us on Earth.

THIS CYCLE REPEATS EVERY ~29.5 DAYS:

Position 1, "New": Each cycle begins with the Moon dark in the sky backlit by the Sun (aka "New", position 1) ...

Positions 2-4, "Waxing": moving counterclockwise, appearing to grow bigger and brighter every day ...

Position 5, "Full": until she appears to be fully illuminated by the sun ...

Positions 6-8, "Waning": the cycle continues as the Moon travels back to her original location, appearing smaller and darker until she is at Position 1, "New", again.

MOON PHASES + CORE ACTIONS

EACH MOON PHASE IS RELATED TO A CORE ACTION.

The New Moon represents beginnings
and the Full Moon represents culminations,
but what about all the phases in between?

THERE ARE 8 MOON PHASES:

4 Primary + 4 Intermediate

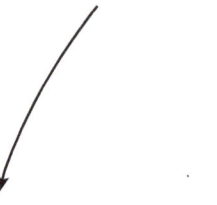

PRIMARY MOON PHASES

Occurs at an exact day + time.

NEW

1ST QUARTER

FULL

LAST QUARTER

INTERMEDIATE MOON PHASES

Occurs over appx. 1 week.

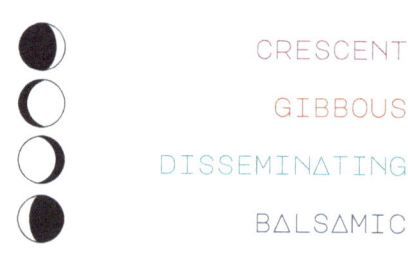

CRESCENT

GIBBOUS

DISSEMINATING

BALSAMIC

TO NOTE: In this planner, Moon Phase transits are
determined by Universal Time, but the following
time zones are noted for New Moons and Full Moons:
Los Angeles, New York, London + Sydney.

Those in the Southern Hemisphere will see Moon Phases in
their sky appearing opposite in respect to pages shown here.

No matter when you start using this planner, there is always
an action to assist you at every point in the cycle.

1. NEW MOON | "NEW MOON" | MANIFEST

Set intentions. Plant seeds.
Identify goals + dreams. Make wishes. Follow your heart.

2. CRESCENT | "WAXING CRESCENT" | PROGRESS

Take action. Trust instincts. Make plans.
Be courageous. Build good habits. Innovate.

3. 1ST QUARTER | "WAXING QUARTER" | MOTIVATE

Renew momentum. Identify challenges.
Reevaluate. Set boundaries. Adjust.

4. GIBBOUS | "WAXING GIBBOUS" | EXPAND

Improve. Recognize luck. Connect.
Notice synchronicities. Tend to health. Listen to self.

5. FULL MOON | "FULL MOON" | ENJOY

Harvest. Heal. Bloom. Have fun. Get creative.
Celebrate progress. Acknowledge growth.

6. DISSEMINATING | "WANING GIBBOUS" | REFLECT

Be appreciative. Share wisdom. Educate. Reveal.
Process. Review boundaries. Write + record.

7. LAST QUARTER | "WANING QUARTER" | RELEASE

Clear the air. Forgive. Surrender.
Embrace calm. Find balance. Clear path.

8. BALSAMIC | "WANING CRESCENT" | RESTORE

Trust intuition. Rest. Dream. Examine ego. Find grace.
Focus on self-care. Clean + Declutter. Self-care.

NEW MOONS

Start of Lunar cycle.
New Beginnings.

The Moon sits between the Earth and the Sun.
From our view, the Moon is backlit,
projecting no light.

A New Moon occurs when the Sun + the Moon
are in the same Zodiac sign.

There are ~12 monthly New Moons each year.
Sometimes there are 13, where 1 month gets 2.
This 13th New Moon shows up once every 2 - 3 years,
and is known as the "Black Moon".

A "Black Moon" is also a 3rd New Moon in a Season of 4 New Moons.
In 2023, there are 12 New Moons - May 19th is a "Black Moon".
.
In very rare cases, a month will not have a New Moon at all,
which happens once every ~19 years + only in February.

A Solar Eclipse only occurs when the Moon is New,
and when the Sun + Earth align with the Moon's Nodes.
When it's New, the Moon blocks the Sun from Earth,
casting her shadow on our surface - making the Sun appear darker.
Rotating sets every ~18 months, eclipses play out the themes of
opposing astrological signs in our karmic and spiritual paths.
Eclipses = 3x the power of New or Full Moons.

During a New Moon you should Connect + Manifest.
Set intentions, make wishes, plant seeds + follow your heart.
Provides ~2 weeks of momentum + acceleration.

Opportunities:
Most potent Phase for intention rituals,
+ most destructive time for magick.
Strong for banishments, divinations, curses + beginnings.

Hazards:
Getting stuck in the past. Exposure to toxicity.

FULL MOONS

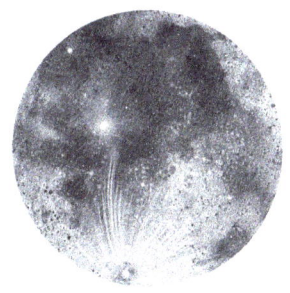

The Earth sits between the Sun and the Moon.
From our view, the Moon is bathing in sunlight,
projecting full light.

A Full Moon occurs when the Sun + the Moon
are in opposite Zodiac signs.

There are ~12 monthly Full Moons each year.
Sometimes there are 13, where 1 month gets 2.
This 13th Full Moon shows up once every 2 - 3 years,
and is known as the "Blue Moon".

A "Blue Moon" is also a 3rd Full Moon in a Season of 4 Full Moons.
In 2023, there are 13 Full Moons - August 31st is a "Blue Moon".

In very rare cases, a month will not have a Full Moon at all,
which happens once every ~19 years + only in February.

A Lunar Eclipse only occurs when the Moon is Full,
and when the Sun + Earth align with the Moon's Nodes.
When it's Full, the Earth blocks the Sun from the Moon,
casting our shadow on her surface - making the Moon appear darker.
Rotating sets every ~18 months, eclipses play out the themes of
opposing astrological signs in our karmic and spiritual paths.
Eclipses = 3x the power of New or Full Moons.

During a Full Moon you should Harvest + Enjoy.
Celebrate progress, have fun, be creative + acknowledge growth.
Provides ~2 weeks of reevaluation + restoration.

Opportunities:
Most potent of all Phases for any rituals,
+ most powerful time for magick.
Strong for protection, manifestation, healing + desires.

Hazards:
Making rash decisions. Emotionally charged overreactions.

FULL MOON NICKNAMES

EACH MONTH'S FULL MOON HAS A SPECIAL NICKNAME.

Because Earth's Moon is a natural timepiece,
the naming of each Full Moon was a way for Native peoples
across the globe to keep time and anticipate the seasons.

Originally named after regional traditions,
climates or environmental factors, the Full Moon's
nickname was largely dependent on where one lived.

For instance, the January Full Moon is largely known as the
"Wolf Moon", named for the hungry, howling wolves of winter.
However, January is also known as the "Ice Moon",
"Old Moon", and "Spirit Moon", to name a few.

To note: the "Harvest Moon" is the Full Moon closest to the
Fall Equinox in either September or October, but adopts
"Corn Moon" or "Hunter's Moon" respectively when it's not.

The most well known Full Moon nicknames were
designated by the Native American Algonquin Tribe,
and are referenced in this Moon Time Planner.

Those in the Southern Hemisphere
can either adopt the opposite month's Moon nickname
(January for July, February for August... and so on),
or research local resources to find the unique
monthly Full Moon nicknames for your specific area.

January
"WOLF MOON"

February
"SNOW MOON"

March
"WORM MOON"

April
"PINK MOON"

May
"FLOWER MOON"

June
"STRAWBERRY MOON"

July
"BUCK MOON"

August
"STURGEON MOON"

September
"CORN / HARVEST MOON"

October
"HUNTER'S / HARVEST MOON"

November
"BEAVER MOON"

December
"COLD MOON"

SETTING MOOD + INTENTIONS

An intention is more than a "wish", but also not a demand or an expectation. An intention is something you feel drawn to or even something that compels you. It can be absolutely anything with no limitations - something quick and easy, or long-term and life-changing. It's up to you. Below are some suggestions to help enhance your mood + intention setting experience. You can also find recommended products at: www.moontimeplanner.com

REMOVE DISTRACTIONS
Silence all non-emergent notifications.
If you live with others consider requesting at least
20 minutes of uninterrupted, alone time. Animals welcome!

CREATE A PERSONAL ALTAR
Either permanent or temporary, choose a protected spot that can exist undisturbed. Adorn the area with things you love: trinkets, heirlooms, photographs, crystals, etc. Consider incorporating natural elements: Earth, Wind, Fire, Water (i.e. feather for Wind, candle for fire, etc).

SET THE MOOD
Play some relaxing music.
Safely light candles and dim the lights.
If weather permits, go outside or open windows for fresh air.

BREW A WARM BEVERAGE
Besides the health benefits of drinking tea,
it also activates your sense of taste, smell and touch.
If you can't drink tea, any warm beverage will do.

CLEANSE YOUR SPACE
Burn incense or sage to help clear out any
negative energy built up over the last Lunar cycle.
Burning sage, aka "smudging", is an Indigenous ritual used
to bring clarity while purifying the mind, body and soul.

CENTER YOURSELF
Take a moment to check in with yourself by taking
a few slow, deep breaths. Consider a short meditation.
If you don't use an app for meditation already,
you can find them available for free on YouTube.

SETTING INTENTIONS
Get your favorite pen and answer the questions
provided for each New Moon in this planner.
After you're finished, get a piece of notebook paper
and restate your intention in one or two simple sentences.

BURN OR BURY INTENTIONS
In a burn-safe container and environment, light your
intentions on fire. If you can't light fire safely,
bury them in the soil of a plant in or around your home.

ASTROLOGY: PLANETS, HOUSES & SIGNS

Astrology is the study of the stars and planets in regard to their relative positions in the sky, with each angle they make to one another carrying various assigned meanings from 12 different categories of life. Presented as a wheel, the fixed outer circle designates "Houses", while the inner circles of Stars + Planets move around (see chart p.17).

(see chart p.17)

You	"WHO"	→ EXACT MOMENT OF BIRTH
Planets	"WHAT"	→ ARCHETYPE ENERGY EXPRESSED
Houses	"WHERE"	→ CATEGORIES WHERE PLANETS RESIDE
Signs	"HOW"	→ TRAITS TO EXPRESS YOURSELF

Astrology was created in Mesopotamia ~3,000 years ago by ancient Babylonians. Originally astronomy before astrology, stars and celestial bodies were tracked and noted along with the seasons. Early astronomers discovered there was a belt-shaped region in the night sky featuring 12 revolving "constellations" (aka Signs) that the Sun, Moon and visible Planets appeared to passed through over the course of 1 solar year. To further make sense of their world and the meaning of life, each Sign was given a series of personality traits relating to a different theme or general expression. Commonly known as the Zodiac aka "circle of little animals", they're listed in order and begin with the arrival of Spring:

Aries, Ram	CONFIDENT	Libra, Scales	HARMONIOUS
Taurus, Bull	SENSUAL	Scorpio, Scorpion	PASSIONATE
Gemini, Twins	SMART	Sagittarius, Archer	CAREFREE
Cancer, Crab	EMOTIONAL	Capricorn, Sea-Goat	ENDURING
Leo, Lion	LOYAL	Aquarius, Water-Bearer	FRIENDLY
Virgo, Maiden	ANALYTICAL	Pisces, Fish	INTUITIVE

Coinciding with the Zodiac is the "House" system. While the Zodiac rotates like a belt and is determined by the apparent position of the Sun, the Houses are fixed and dependent on Earth's 24-hour rotation on it's own axis. Represented by a wheel, the 12 Houses are numbered and associated with major life categories. Babylonians believed that our life purpose was determined by our exact time and place of birth. The Rising Sign (aka Ascendant) is the Sign rising on Earth's eastern horizon at the moment we are born (1st House) - which appears at the 9 o'clock position. Moving counterclockwise around the wheel, the Houses are as follows:

1st House	SELF	7th House	BALANCE
2nd House	VALUE	8th House	TRANSFORMATION
3rd House	SHARING	9th House	PURPOSE
4th House	HOME	10th House	ENTERPRISE
5th House	PLEASURE	11th House	COMMUNITY
6th House	HEALTH	12th House	SACRIFICE

Populating the Signs and the Houses are the Planets. When ancient astronomers studied the night sky, they noticed 5 stars wandering around amongst the fixed constellations and named them after their Gods. Each Planet is therefore associated with a Deity archetype. In modern astrology there are 8 Planets + the Sun and Moon:

Sun	THE EGO	Jupiter	THE GROWTH
Moon	THE EMOTIONS	Saturn	THE DISCIPLINE
Mercury	THE COMMUNICATION	Uranus	THE CHAOS
Venus	THE LOVE	Neptune	THE FANTASY
Mars	THE ACTIONS	Pluto	THE POWER

ASTROLOGY: READING NATAL CHARTS

This is optional - you don't need to know anything about your personal Natal Chart to use this planner. However, if you want deeper insights, you can generate one for free online by plugging in your birth date, birth time and birth location. Most free sites provide a detailed breakdown as well.

Getting your exact birth time is vital - not only do the Houses rely on it, but Rising Signs change every 2 hours and the Moon shifts every 2-3 days. If you aren't sure, grab your birth certificate, ask a parent, or call the hospital where you were born. If none of those options work, use 12 noon for a max error of only +/- 12 hours. Although your Houses, Rising and Moon will be unreliable, you'll at least get Signs, Planets and the angles they form (aka Aspects).

The Natal Chart is a circle - 360°. The outer rim denotes the Houses, the middle wheel contains the Signs, and the inner portion is populated by the Planets. When your birth info is entered, the wheel containing the Signs will rotate, and the Planets will scatter to a specific degree. In the chart shown here, the 12 Houses, 12 Signs and 10 Planets/Celestial Bodies are in their home positions.

The 12 Houses (p.15) are divided into fixed positions on the outer circle. Think of Houses 1-6 as "below the horizon", and Houses 7-12 as "above the horizon". Houses below are deemed "Personal" (ego, values, health, etc), while Houses above are "Interpersonal" (relationships, career, community, etc). Houses opposite each other sit on an axis that highlight their polarity (i.e. 4th House of Home/Private Life vs. 10th House of Enterprise/Public Life).

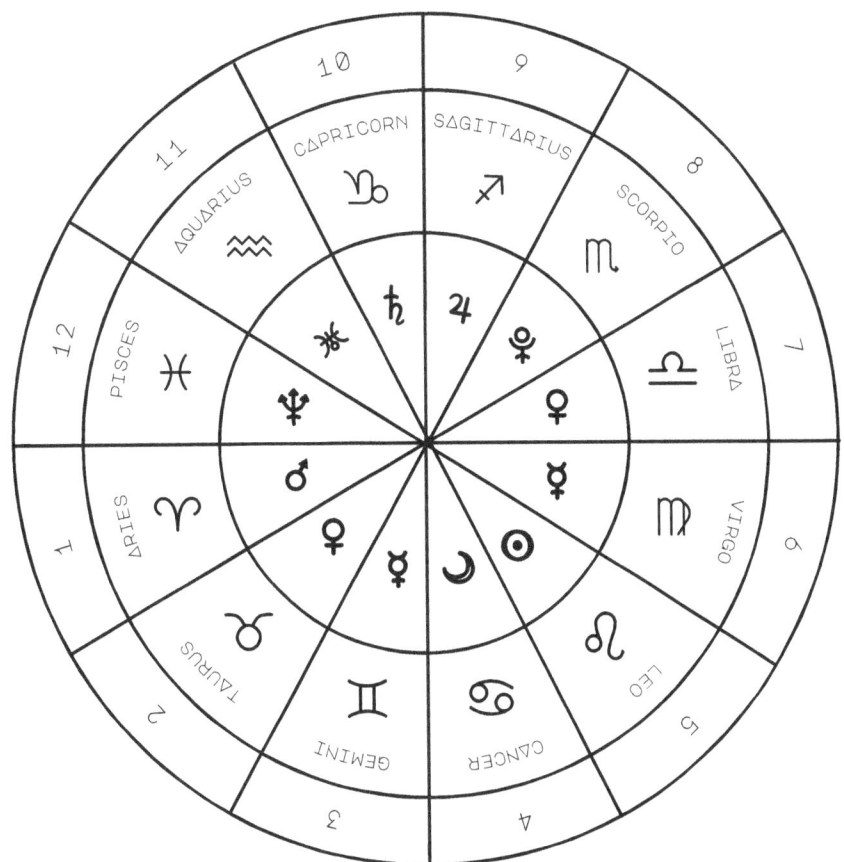

The Planets (p.15) are archetypes playing out themes in your Houses, and the Signs (p.14) are how you express yourself in that combo (i.e. a person with Aries + Mars in their 1st House broadly implies that their sense of self is largely based in ego, which is expressed with self-confidence.

The 3 most important personal Signs are your Sun, Moon and Rising. Sun Signs change monthly, Moon Signs switch every 2-3 days and Rising Signs shift every 2 hours. Your Rising is found on your Natal Chart where House 1 + House 12 meet. The Sun = core identity, Moon = emotions and Rising = the way you act in the world. For horoscopes, consult your Rising > Sun.

Aspects are the angles formed by Signs + Planets sitting at various degrees and categorized as favorable / easy (60° Sextile, 120° Trine), unfavorable/hard (90° Square, 180° Opposition), or close/energizing (>10° Conjunct).

ASTROLOGY: QUICK GUIDE

ARIES | MAR. 21 - APR. 19

Ruled by Mars + 1st House
Confident. Motivated.
Active. Impulsive.
Headstrong. Brave.

TAURUS | APR. 20 - MAY 20

Ruled by Venus + 2nd House
Sensual. Secure.
Steadfast. Stubborn.
Luxurious. Hard working.

GEMINI | MAY. 21 - JUN. 20

Ruled by Mercury + 3rd House
Smart. Communicative.
Social. Gossipy.
Chatty. Witty.

CANCER | JUN. 21 - JUL. 22

Ruled by the Moon + 4th House
Emotional. Nurturing.
Compassionate. Moody.
Caring. Safe.

LEO | JUL. 23 - AUG. 22

Ruled by the Sun + 5th House
Loyal. Generous.
Glamorous. Dramatic.
Charismatic. Fun-loving.

VIRGO | AUG. 23 - SEPT. 22

Ruled by Mercury + 6th House
Analytical. Precise.
Practical. Critical.
Organized. Controlling.

LIBRA | SEPT. 23 - OCT. 22

Ruled by Venus + 7th House
Harmonious. Balanced.
Tactful. Indecisive.
Conciliatory. Peaceful.

SCORPIO | OCT. 23 - NOV. 21

Ruled by Pluto + 8th House
Passionate. Transformative.
Cunning. Extreme.
Sexual. Investigative.

SAGITTARIUS | NOV. 22 - DEC. 21

Ruled by Jupiter + 9th House
Carefree. Optimistic.
Expansive. Blunt.
Humorous. Wandering.

CAPRICORN | DEC. 22 - JAN. 19

Ruled by Saturn + 10th House
Enduring. Ambitious.
Determined. Ruthless.
Materialistic. Successful.

AQUARIUS | JAN. 20 - FEB. 18

Ruled by Uranus + 11th House
Friendly. Progressive.
Inventive. Detached.
Restless. Independent.

PISCES | FEB. 19 - MAR. 20

Ruled by Neptune + 12th House
Intuitive. Psychic.
Creative. Escapist.
Wise. Spiritual.

HOW TO USE THIS PLANNER

FEB 2023		MONDAY	TUESDAY	WEDNESDAY
WEEK 5				1
		WEEK NUMBER COLUMN Use these boxes to account for top tasks or goals each week		WAXING GIBBOUS →
WEEK 6		6	7	8
			WANING DISSEMINATING →	
WEEK 7		13	14	15
		SCORPIO LAST QUARTER	WANING BALSAMIC →	
WEEK 8		20	21	22
		PISCES SUPER NEW MOON	WAXING CRESCENT →	
WEEK 9		27	28	
		GEMINI 1ST QUARTER	WAXING GIBBOUS →	

HABITS	GOAL	1	2	3	4	5	6	7	8	9	10	11	12	13	14	15	16	17	18
						HABIT TRACKER Use this space to set monthly goals for habits and track your progress every day													

THURSDAY	FRIDAY	SATURDAY	SUNDAY
2	3	4	5
			○ ♌ ✴ LEO FULL MOON "SNOW MOON"
9	10	11	
		SYMBOLS — The 4 Primary Moon Phases are noted, along with the Moon's current Astrological sign. Additional insight provided on Daily Calendar pages	
16	17	18	19
		SUN → PISCES	
23	24	25	26
		TRANSIT TRACKERS: — Refer to these boxes for quick reference of the Primary Moon Phases + Planetary Transits	

19	20	21	22	23	24	25	26	27	28	29	32	31	TOTAL

MOON PHASES:

2/05
FULL MOON

2/13
LAST QUARTER

2/20
SUPER
NEW MOON

2/27
1ST QUARTER

KEY DATES:

2/18
SUN → PISCES

HOW TO USE THIS PLANNER

JAN.01,'23

SUNDAY | WEEK 52

TOP TASKS:
- [ ]
- [ ] DAILY MOON PHASE & MOON SIGN
- [ ] Tracks Moon Phase + Astrological Transits

TRACKING:

PERSONAL TRACKING

Your box to track unique items

DAILY GRATITUDE:

GOLD STAR DAY

Color in the star as reward
for having a good day!

6		2	
7		3	
8		4	
9		5	DAY PLANNER
10		6	Plan your hourly schedule in detail
11		7	
12		8	
1		9	

GIBBOUS MOON, WAXING / EXPAND:

What is something giving
you hope right now?

MOOD:

MOOD TRACKING

Your box to track daily mood

LUNAR-GUIDED JOURNAL PROMPT

Designed for each day's specific Moon Phase

MOON PHASE ACTION REMINDER

The start of each Moon Phase is featured
here to inspire intentional action.

Gibbous Moon: Expand. Recognize luck.
Reconnect with intentions. Tend to emotions. Improve.

DAILY CALENDAR VIEW

JAN.02,'23

MONDAY | WEEK 01

TRACKING:

☆

TOP TASKS:

☐
☐
☐

TOP 3 TO-DO'S
Keep track of important tasks

DAILY GRATITUDE:

SHOW APPRECIATION
Studies show gratitude increases success

6		2	
7		3	
8		4	
9		5	
10		6	
11		7	
12		8	
1		9	

GIBBOUS MOON, WAXING / EXPAND:
What is something you're
looking forward to?

MOOD:

MAJOR PLANETARY EVENTS
will be noted here

NOTES SECTION
Use this space to answer journal prompts
or for personal notes + creativity.

ZODIAC SYMBOL
Zodiac symbol of the sign
the Moon is currently in.

MOON TIME PLANNER

JANUARY 1ST - JUNE 30TH, 2023

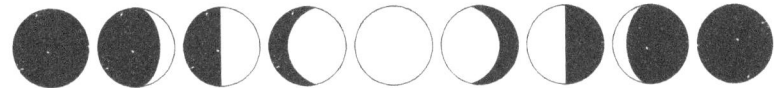

STATE-OF-SELF CHECK-IN

Based on the Astrological Houses (p.15), rate each area of your life 1-10 and make notes in the space provided. Identify areas which deserve attention, improvement + appreciation.

How do I feel about myself?   1 2 3 4 5 6 7 8 9 10

How stable is my life?   1 2 3 4 5 6 7 8 9 10

How is my communication?   1 2 3 4 5 6 7 8 9 10

How is my home life?   1 2 3 4 5 6 7 8 9 10

How much am I enjoying myself?   1 2 3 4 5 6 7 8 9 10

How is my physical health?   1 2 3 4 5 6 7 8 9 10

How are my relationships?   1 2 3 4 5 6 7 8 9 10

_____

_____

_____

How am I coping with change?   1 2 3 4 5 6 7 8 9 10

_____

_____

_____

How much am I learning?   1 2 3 4 5 6 7 8 9 10

_____

_____

_____

How is my reputation / career?   1 2 3 4 5 6 7 8 9 10

_____

_____

_____

How are my friendships / community?   1 2 3 4 5 6 7 8 9 10

_____

_____

_____

How is my sleep / self-care?   1 2 3 4 5 6 7 8 9 10

_____

_____

_____

Areas of Attention and Appreciation Over Next 3 Months:

_____

_____

_____

2023

13 FULL MOONS = ○ ● = 12 NEW MOONS

1/06	★	2/05	★	3/07	
4/06	★	5/05	★	6/04	
7/03	★	8/01	★	8/31	
9/29	★	10/28	★	11/27 ★ 12/26	

1/21	★	2/20	★	3/21	
4/20	★	5/19	★	6/18	
7/17	★	8/16	★	9/15	
10/14	★	11/13	★	12/12	

JANUARY

M	T	W	T	F	S	S
30	31					1
2	3	4	5	6 ○	7	8
9	10	11	12	13	14	15
16	17	18	19	20	21 ●	22
23	24	25	26	27	28	29

FEBRUARY

M	T	W	T	F	S	S
		1	2	3	4	5 ○
6	7	8	9	10	11	12
13	14	15	16	17	18	19
20 ●	21	22	23	24	25	26
27	28					

MARCH

M	T	W	T	F	S	S
		1	2	3	4	5
6	7 ○	8	9	10	11	12
13	14	15	16	17	18	19
20	21 ●	22	23	24	25	26
27	28	29	30	31		

APRIL

M	T	W	T	F	S	S
					1	2
3	4	5	6 ○	7	8	9
10	11	12	13	14	15	16
17	18	19	20 ●	21	22	23
24	25	26	27	28	29	30

MAY

M	T	W	T	F	S	S
1	2	3	4	5 ○	6	7
8	9	10	11	12	13	14
15	16	17	18	19 ●	20	21
22	23	24	25	26	27	28
29	30	31				

JUNE

M	T	W	T	F	S	S
			1	2	3	4 ○
5	6	7	8	9	10	11
12	13	14	15	16	17	18 ●
19	20	21	22	23	24	25
26	27	28	29	30		

5 SPECIAL MOONS = ☀

1/21	★	Super New Moon	
2/20	★	Super New Moon	
5/19	★	Black New Moon	
8/01	★	Super Full Moon	
8/31	★	Super Blue Moon	

☽ = 4 ECLIPSES

Aries	★	Solar	★	4/20
Scorpio	★	Lunar	★	5/05
		&		
Libra	★	Solar	★	10/14
Taurus	★	Lunar	★	10/28

2023

JULY

M	T	W	T	F	S	S
31					1	2
3 ○	4	5	6	7	8	9
10	11	12	13	14	15	16
17 ●	18	19	20	21	22	23
24	25	26	27	28	29	30

AUGUST

M	T	W	T	F	S	S
	1 ○ ☀	2	3	4	5	6
7	8	9	10	11	12	13
14	15	16 ●	17	18	19	20
21	22	23	24	25	26	27
28	29	30	31 ○ ☀			

SEPTEMBER

M	T	W	T	F	S	S
				1	2	3
4	5	6	7	8	9	10
11	12	13	14	15 ●	16	17
18	19	20	21	22	23	24
25	26	27	28	29 ○	30	

OCTOBER

M	T	W	T	F	S	S
30	31					1
2	3	4	5	6	7	8
9	10	11	12	13	14 ● ☽	15
16	17	18	19	20	21	22
23	24	25	26	27	28 ○ ☽	29

NOVEMBER

M	T	W	T	F	S	S
		1	2	3	4	5
6	7	8	9	10	11	12
13 ●	14	15	16	17	18	19
20	21	22	23	24	25	26
27 ○	28	29	30			

DECEMBER

M	T	W	T	F	S	S
				1	2	3
4	5	6	7	8	9	10
11	12 ●	13	14	15	16	17
18	19	20	21	22	23	24
25	26 ○	27	28	29	30	31

JANUARY 2023	MONDAY	TUESDAY	WEDNESDAY
WEEK 52	30 (WEEK 5)	31 (WEEK 5)	
WEEK 1	2	3	4
		VENUS → AQUARIUS	
WEEK 2	9	10	11
WEEK 3	16	17	18
	WANING BALSAMIC →		MERCURY DIRECT →
WEEK 4	23	24	25
	WAXING CRESCENT →		

HABITS	GOAL	1	2	3	4	5	6	7	8	9	10	11	12	13	14	15	16	17	18

THURSDAY	FRIDAY	SATURDAY	SUNDAY
			1
			HAPPY NEW YEAR! WAXING GIBBOUS → MERCURY RETROGRADE →
5	6	7	8
	○ ♋ CANCER FULL MOON "WOLF MOON"		WANING DISSEMINATING →
12	13	14	15
MARS DIRECT →			◐ ♎ LIBRA LAST QUARTER
19	20	21	22
	☼ ♒ SUN → AQUARIUS	● ♒ ✳ AQUARIUS SUPER NEW MOON	URANUS DIRECT →
26	27	28	29
	VENUS → PISCES	◑ ♉ TAURUS 1ST QUARTER	WAXING GIBBOUS →

19	20	21	22	23	24	25	26	27	28	29	30	31	TOTAL

MOON PHASES:

1/06
Full Moon

1/15
Last Quarter

1/21
Super New Moon

1/28
1st Quarter

KEY MOMENTS:

1/20
Sun → Aquarius

1/12
Mars Direct →

1/18
Mercury Direct →

1/22
Uranus Direct →

FEBRUARY 2023	MONDAY	TUESDAY	WEDNESDAY
WEEK 5			1
			WAXING GIBBOUS →
WEEK 6	6	7	8
		WANING DISSEMINATING →	
WEEK 7	13	14	15
	◐ ♏ SCORPIO LAST QUARTER	WANING BALSAMIC →	
WEEK 8	20	21	22
	● ♓ ✳ PISCES SUPER NEW MOON VENUS → ARIES	WAXING CRESCENT →	
WEEK 9	27	28	
	◐ ♊ GEMINI 1ST QUARTER	WAXING GIBBOUS →	

HABITS	GOAL	1	2	3	4	5	6	7	8	9	10	11	12	13	14	15	16	17	18

THURSDAY	FRIDAY	SATURDAY	SUNDAY
2	3	4	5 ○ ♌ LEO FULL MOON "SNOW MOON"
9	10	11 MERCURY → AQUARIUS	12
16	17	18 ♓ SUN → PISCES	19
23	24	25	26

19	20	21	22	23	24	25	26	27	28	29	30	31	TOTAL

MOON PHASES:

2/05
Full Moon

2/13
Last Quarter

2/20
Super New Moon

2/27
1st Quarter

KEY MOMENTS:

2/18
Sun → Pisces

MARCH 2023	MONDAY	TUESDAY	WEDNESDAY
WEEK 10			1
			WAXING GIBBOUS →
WEEK 11	6	7	8
		◯ ♍ VIRGO FULL MOON "WORM MOON" SATURN → PISCES	♍ WANING DISSEMINATING →
WEEK 12	13	14	15
			◐ ♐ SAGITTARIUS LAST QUARTER
WEEK 13	20	21	22
	☀ ♈ SUN → ARIES SPRING EQUINOX	● ♈ ARIES NEW MOON	
WEEK 14	27	28	29
			◑ ♋ CANCER 1ST QUARTER

HABITS	GOAL	1	2	3	4	5	6	7	8	9	10	11	12	13	14	15	16	17	18

THURSDAY	FRIDAY	SATURDAY	SUNDAY
2	3	4	5
MERCURY → PISCES			
9	10	11	12
			JUPITER ♥ CHIRON
16	17	18	19
WANING BALSAMIC → VENUS → TAURUS			MERCURY → ARIES
23	24	25	26
WAXING CRESCENT → PLUTO → AQUARIUS		MARS → CANCER	
30	31		
WAXING GIBBOUS →			

19	20	21	22	23	24	25	26	27	28	29	30	31	TOTAL

MOON PHASES:

3/07
Full Moon

3/15
Last Quarter

3/21
Super New Moon

3/29
1st Quarter

KEY MOMENTS:

3/07
Saturn → Pisces

3/12
Jupiter ♥ Chiron

3/23
Pluto → Aquarius

3/20
Sun → Aries

3/20
Spring Equinox

ΔPRIL 2023	MONDΔY	TUESDΔY	WEDNESDΔY
WEEK 15			
WEEK 16	3	4	5
	MERCURY → TΔURUS		
WEEK 17	10	11	12
		VENUS → GEMINI	
WEEK 18	17	18	19
WEEK 19	24	25	26

HΔBITS	GOΔL	1	2	3	4	5	6	7	8	9	10	11	12	13	14	15	16	17	18

THURSDAY	FRIDAY	SATURDAY	SUNDAY
		1	2
		WAXING GIBBOUS →	
6	7	8	9
♎︎ LIBRA FULL MOON "PINK MOON"	WANING DISSEMINATING →		
13	14	15	16
♑︎ CAPRICORN LAST QUARTER	WANING BALSAMIC →		
20	21	22	23
♉︎ ♈︎ ARIES NEW MOON SOLAR ECLIPSE SUN → TAURUS	WAXING CRESCENT → MERCURY RETROGRADE →		
27	28	29	30
♌︎ LEO 1ST QUARTER	WAXING GIBBOUS →		

19	20	21	22	23	24	25	26	27	28	29	30	31	TOTAL

MOON PHASES:

4/06
Full Moon

4/13
Last Quarter

4/20
New Moon
Solar Eclipse

4/27
1st Quarter

KEY MOMENTS:

4/20
Sun → Taurus

4/21
Mercury
Retrograde →

MΔY 2023	MONDΔY	TUESDΔY	WEDNESDΔY
WEEK 20	1	2	3
	WΔXING GIBBOUS → PLUTO RETROGRΔDE →		
WEEK 21	8	9	10
WEEK 22	15	16	17
	MERCURY DIRECT →	JUPITER → TΔURUS	
WEEK 23	22	23	24
WEEK 24	29	30	31

HΔBITS	GOΔL	1	2	3	4	5	6	7	8	9	10	11	12	13	14	15	16	17	18

THURSDAY	FRIDAY	SATURDAY	SUNDAY
4	5 ○ ♏ ☽ SCORPIO FULL MOON LUNAR ECLIPSE "FLOWER MOON"	6	7 WANING DISSEMINATING → VENUS → CANCER
11	12 ◑ ♒ AQUARIUS LAST QUARTER	13 WANING BALSAMIC →	14
18 JUPITER ⊗ PLUTO	19 ● ♉ ✳ TAURUS BLACK NEW MOON	20 MARS → LEO	21 ♊ WAXING CRESCENT → SUN → GEMINI
25	26	27 ◐ ♍ VIRGO 1ST QUARTER	28 WAXING GIBBOUS →

19	20	21	22	23	24	25	26	27	28	29	30	31	TOTAL

MOON PHASES:

5/05
Full Moon
Lunar Eclipse

5/12
Last Quarter

5/19
Black New Moon

5/27
1st Quarter

KEY MOMENTS:

5/01
Pluto Retro →

5/15
Mercury Direct →

5/16
Jupiter → Taurus

5/18
Jupiter ⊗ Pluto

5/21
Sun → Gemini

JUNE 2023	MONDAY	TUESDAY	WEDNESDAY
WEEK 25			
WEEK 26	5	6	7
	WANING DISSEMINATING → VENUS → LEO		
WEEK 27	12	13	14
WEEK 28	19	20	21
	WAXING CRESCENT → JUPITER ♥ SATURN		♋ SUN → CANCER SUMMER SOLSTICE
WEEK 29	26	27	28
	♎ LIBRA 1ST QUARTER MERCURY → CANCER	WAXING GIBBOUS →	

HABITS	GOAL	1	2	3	4	5	6	7	8	9	10	11	12	13	14	15	16	17	18

THURSDAY	FRIDAY	SATURDAY	SUNDAY
1	2	3	4
WAXING GIBBOUS →			○ ♐ SAGITTARIUS FULL MOON "STRAWBERRY MOON"
8	9	10	11
		◑ ♓ PISCES LAST QUARTER	WANING BALSAMIC → PLUTO → CAPRICORN MERCURY → GEMINI
15	16	17	18
		SATURN RETROGRADE →	● ♊ GEMINI NEW MOON
22	23	24	25
29	30	31	
	NEPTUNE RETROGRADE →		

19	20	21	22	23	24	25	26	27	28	29	30	31	TOTAL

MOON PHASES:

6/04
Full Moon

6/10
Last Quarter

6/18
Super New Moon

6/26
1st Quarter

KEY MOMENTS:

6/21
Sun → Cancer

6/21
Summer Solstice

6/17
Saturn Retro →

6/30
Neptune Retro →

6/21
Jupiter ♥ Saturn

JAN.01,'23

SUNDAY | WEEK 52

☆

TOP TASKS:
☐
☐
☐

DAILY GRATITUDE:

6	2
7	3
8	4
9	5
10	6
11	7
12	8
1	9

GIBBOUS MOON, WAXING / EXPAND:

What is something giving
you hope right now?

MOOD:

Gibbous Moon: Expand. Improve. Recognize luck. Connect.
Notice synchronicities. Tend to health. Listen to self.

JAN.02,'23
MONDAY | WEEK 1

☾ ♉

☆

TOP TASKS:
- ☐
- ☐
- ☐

DAILY GRATITUDE:

6	2
7	3
8	4
9	5
10	6
11	7
12	8
1	9

GIBBOUS MOON, WAXING / EXPAND:

What can you do to motivate yourself?

MOOD:

☾ ♉ ♊

TRACKING:

☆

TOP TASKS:
- [ ]
- [ ]
- [ ]

DAILY GRATITUDE:

6	2
7	3
8	4
9	5
10	6
11	7
12	8
1	9

GIBBOUS MOON, WAXING / EXPAND:
What is something
you're looking forward to?

MOOD:

VENUS → AQUARIUS

JAN.04,'23
WEDNESDAY | WEEK 1

♉ Gemini ⚋

TRACKING:

☆

TOP TASKS:
- [ ]
- [ ]
- [ ]

DAILY GRATITUDE:

6	2
7	3
8	4
9	5
10	6
11	7
12	8
1	9

GIBBOUS MOON, WAXING / EXPAND:
Where could you be
saving money or resources?

MOOD:

JAN.05,'23
THURSDAY | WEEK 1

♊ ♋

☆

TOP TASKS:
- [ ]
- [ ]
- [ ]

DAILY GRATITUDE:

6	2
7	3
8	4
9	5
10	6
11	7
12	8
1	9

GIBBOUS MOON, WAXING / EXPAND:
In what ways could you
be communicating better?

MOOD:

CANCER FULL MOON

"WOLF MOON" | JANUARY 06, 2023

The 1st Full Moon of 2023 is in the sensitive sign of Cancer.

Ruled by the Moon herself, we kick off 2023 by getting nostalgic, reflecting on 2022, celebrating wins, and releasing what no longer serves us.

Cancer is all about the home, family, chosen family, comfort, compassion + emotional safety. This Full Moon encourages us to find gratitude for what we call home + who we call home.

Opposite the Full Moon is the Sun in Capricorn, which is all about career, reputation + societal status. Therefore, the Cancer-Capricorn Sun-Moon duality challenges us to balance our private lives vs. our public lives.

Graciousness is an especially helpful trait right now with Mercury (communication) in Retrograde through 01.18. Highlighting errors in our conversations + connections, strive to find grace for the people you love and remember where others have extended that same grace to you. Also in Retrograde is Mars (action), reminding us to reevaluate how we react. With 2 major Retrogrades and a highly emotional Full Moon, it would be wise to avoid confrontations and review your personal boundaries.

A delicate Full Moon such as this begs for cozy activities, like curling up on the sofa with a good book or throwing on your favorite song while cooking. This is also a perfect Full Moon for a ceremony with your favorite witches.

Set the mood (page 12), then take time to respond to the Full Moon worksheet on the following pages.

What three words best define your 2022 and why?

Describe the wins you're most proud of from 2022:

Which habits did you build (or break) in 2022?

Describe what you've learned about yourself in 2022:

Imagine your ideal 2023 and detail it here:

What are you releasing this Full Moon and why?

♋

TRACKING:

☆

TOP TASKS:
☐
☐
☐

DAILY GRATITUDE:

6		2
7		3
8		4
9		5
10		6
11		7
12		8
1		9

FULL MOON, HARVEST (LA, NY, LON):
Take time to complete the Full Moon
worksheet on the previous pages.

MOOD:

Full Moon: Enjoy. Harvest. Heal. Bloom. Have fun.
Get creative. Celebrate progress. Acknowledge growth.

♋

☆

TOP TASKS:
- ☐
- ☐
- ☐

DAILY GRATITUDE:

6

7

8

9

10

11

12

1

2

3

4

5

6

7

8

9

FULL MOON, HARVEST (SYD):

Celebrate your growth and your wins!

MOOD:

JAN.08,'23
SUNDAY | WEEK 1

○ ♋ ♌

TRACKING:

☆

TOP TASKS:
- ☐
- ☐
- ☐

DAILY GRATITUDE:

6	2
7	3
8	4
9	5
10	6
11	7
12	8
1	9

DISSEMINATING MOON, WANING / REFLECT:
Describe a recent situation
that you feel you handled well.

MOOD:

Disseminating Moon: Reflect. Be appreciative.
Reveal. Process. Review boundaries. Write + record.

JAN.09,'23

♌

TRACKING:

TOP TASKS:

- [ ]
- [ ]
- [ ]

DAILY GRATITUDE:

6		2	
7		3	
8		4	
9		5	
10		6	
11		7	
12		8	
1		9	

DISSEMINATING MOON. WANING / REFLECT:
What is something you started
that needs to be finished?

MOOD:

TRACKING:

TOP TASKS:
☐
☐
☐

DAILY GRATITUDE:

6		2
7		3
8		4
9		5
10		6
11		7
12		8
1		9

DISSEMINATING MOON, WANING / REFLECT:

Breakdown something stopping you
which requires deeper analysis.

MOOD:

JAN.11,'23

WEDNESDAY | WEEK 2

♌ ♍

TRACKING:

☆

TOP TASKS:
- ☐
- ☐
- ☐

DAILY GRATITUDE:

6		2
7		3
8		4
9		5
10		6
11		7
12		8
1		9

DISSEMINATING MOON. WANING / REFLECT:

How can you share something
beneficial with your community?

MOOD:

♍

TRACKING:

☆

TOP TASKS:
☐
☐
☐

DAILY GRATITUDE:

6		2	
7		3	
8		4	
9		5	
10		6	
11		7	
12		8	
1		9	

DISSEMINATING MOON, WANING / REFLECT:

Which relationships have
you counted on lately?

MOOD:

MARS DIRECT

JAN.13,'23

☽ ♍ ♎

TRACKING:

☆

TOP TASKS:
- [ ]
- [ ]
- [ ]

DAILY GRATITUDE:

6	2
7	3
8	4
9	5
10	6
11	7
12	8
1	9

DISSEMINATING MOON. WANING / REFLECT:
What is making you feel doubt or
fear and how can you change it?

MOOD:

JAN.14,'23
SATURDAY | WEEK 2

☆

TOP TASKS:
- ☐
- ☐
- ☐

DAILY GRATITUDE:

6		2	
7		3	
8		4	
9		5	
10		6	
11		7	
12		8	
1		9	

DISSEMINATING MOON, REFLECT / WANING:
Review your boundaries — what healthy adjustments can you make?

MOOD:

JAN.15,'23

SUNDAY | WEEK 2

☽ ♎ ♏

☆

TOP TASKS:
- ☐
- ☐
- ☐

DAILY GRATITUDE:

6		2	
7		3	
8		4	
9		5	
10		6	
11		7	
12		8	
1		9	

LAST QUARTER MOON, RELEASE:

What can you forgive and let go of?

MOOD:

Last Quarter Moon: Release. Clear the air. Forgive.
Surrender. Embrace calm. Find balance. Clear path.

JAN.16,'23
MONDAY | WEEK 3 ◖ ♏

☆

TOP TASKS:
- [ ]
- [ ]
- [ ]

DAILY GRATITUDE:

6		2	
7		3	
8		4	
9		5	
10		6	
11		7	
12		8	
1		9	

BALSAMIC MOON, WANING / RESTORE:
What recent wins
are you happy about?

MOOD:

Balsamic Moon: Restore. Trust intuition. Rest. Dream.
Examine ego. Find grace. Clean + declutter. Self-care.

JAN.17,'23
TUESDAY | WEEK 3

♏ ↗

TRACKING:

☆

TOP TASKS:
- ☐
- ☐
- ☐

DAILY GRATITUDE:

6		2	
7		3	
8		4	
9		5	
10		6	
11		7	
12		8	
1		9	

BALSAMIC MOON, WANING / RESTORE:
Is there anything
you want to quit?

MOOD:

JAN.18,'23

WEDNESDAY | WEEK 3

TOP TASKS:

- ☐
- ☐
- ☐

DAILY GRATITUDE:

6		2	
7		3	
8		4	
9		5	
10		6	
11		7	
12		8	
1		9	

BALSAMIC MOON, WANING / RESTORE:

What is a piece of advice
you want to give yourself?

MOOD:

MERCURY DIRECT

JAN.19,'23
THURSDAY | WEEK 3

↗ ♑

☆

TOP TASKS:
- [ ]
- [ ]
- [ ]

DAILY GRATITUDE:

6		2	
7		3	
8		4	
9		5	
10		6	
11		7	
12		8	
1		9	

BALSAMIC MOON, RESTORE / WANING:
What can you do to connect deeper with your spiritual side?

MOOD:

JAN.20,'23

FRIDAY | WEEK 3

♑

TRACKING:

☆

TOP TASKS:

☐

☐

☐

DAILY GRATITUDE:

6	2
7	3
8	4
9	5
10	6
11	7
12	8
1	9

BALSAMIC MOON, RESTORE / WANING:

Which habits can you continue
(or start) this next Lunar Cycle?

MOOD:

SUN → AQUARIUS ☀

AQUARIUS SUPER NEW MOON

JANUARY 21, 2023

The 1st New Moon of 2023 is in the unique sign of Aquarius.

Also a Supermoon, this New Moon is 3x more powerful than a regular New Moon. It's a perfect time for getting in touch with your best intentions, and setting both long-term and short-term goals for the entire year ahead.

Aquarius is all about friendship, community, progress, invention, detachment, forward-thinking + humanitarian efforts. This New Moon encourages us to start something new, engage in group activities + discover innovative solutions. Centering on unique possibilities, this is your time to think big + be hopeful.

Supporting "big + hopeful" is Jupiter/Aries (growth), vibing with this New Moon (extra powerful for anyone with an Aries Rising). Jupiter is known as the "Great Benefactor", bringing us the potential for luck + opportunity - a helpful combo for any new endeavor. Stay positive, keep a healthy ego and lean into what makes you, *you*.

Aquarius is also known for a certain level of detachment, so consider reviewing your boundaries + breaking bad habits. Moon in Aquarius isn't the best for heavy emotions (if you can help it), so consider low-key hangs with friends instead.

A powerful Super New Moon such as this inspirits us to collaborate with others, in person and digitally, as the Internet is also ruled by Aquarius. No matter where you find friendship or community, you are poised for success.

Set the mood (page 12), then take time to respond to the New Moon worksheet on the following pages.

Dream big: what goals would you like to accomplish in 2023?

What resources do you need to make your goals a reality?

What is your deepest desire – the goal of all goals?

Review your emotional boundaries - where you can improve?

Write down some goals you'd like to work on this Lunar Cycle:

Write out a clear intention for this New Moon:

♑ ♒

TRACKING:

☆

TOP TASKS:
- ☐
- ☐
- ☐

DAILY GRATITUDE:

6		2	
7		3	
8		4	
9		5	
10		6	
11		7	
12		8	
1		9	

SUPER NEW MOON, MANIFEST (LA, NY, LON): Take time to complete the New Moon worksheet on previous pages.

MOOD:

New Moon: Manifest. Set intentions. Plant Seeds.
Follow heart. Identify goals + dreams for the new cycle.

TRACKING:

☆

TOP TASKS:
- [ ]
- [ ]
- [ ]

DAILY GRATITUDE:

6		2	
7		3	
8		4	
9		5	
10		6	
11		7	
12		8	
1		9	

SUPER NEW MOON, MANIFEST (SYD):

Meditate on new or
revived intentions today.

MOOD:

URANUS DIRECT

JAN.23,'23
MONDAY | WEEK 4

≋ ♓

☆

TOP TASKS:
- [ ]
- [ ]
- [ ]

DAILY GRATITUDE:

6		2	
7		3	
8		4	
9		5	
10		6	
11		7	
12		8	
1		9	

CRESCENT MOON, PROGRESS / WAXING:
What's 1 small action you can
take to kick off your intentions?

MOOD:

Crescent Moon: Progress. Take Action. Trust instincts.
Make plans. Be courageous. Build good habits. Innovate.

JAN.24,'23

♓

TRACKING:

☆

TOP TASKS:
- ☐
- ☐
- ☐

DAILY GRATITUDE:

6

7

8

9

10

11

12

1

2

3

4

5

6

7

8

9

CRESCENT MOON, WAXING / PROGRESS:
Which of your strengths
can help you right now?

MOOD:

♓ ♈

TRACKING:

☆

TOP TASKS:
- [ ]
- [ ]
- [ ]

DAILY GRATITUDE:

6

7

8

9

10

11

12

1

2

3

4

5

6

7

8

9

CRESCENT MOON, WAXING / PROGRESS:
What's distracting you from getting
things done + how can you fix it?

MOOD:

♈

TRACKING:

☆

TOP TASKS:
- ☐
- ☐
- ☐

DAILY GRATITUDE:

6		2	
7		3	
8		4	
9		5	
10		6	
11		7	
12		8	
1		9	

CRESCENT MOON, WAXING / PROGRESS:
What kind of research can you
do to support your intentions?

MOOD:

JAN.27,'23

♈ ♉

TRACKING:

☆

TOP TASKS:
- [ ]
- [ ]
- [ ]

DAILY GRATITUDE:

6		2	
7		3	
8		4	
9		5	
10		6	
11		7	
12		8	
1		9	

CRESCENT MOON, WAXING / PROGRESS:
How can you improve your
morning and evening routines?

MOOD:

VENUS → PISCES

TRACKING:

TOP TASKS:
- ☐
- ☐
- ☐

DAILY GRATITUDE:

6		2	
7		3	
8		4	
9		5	
10		6	
11		7	
12		8	
1		9	

1ST QUARTER MOON, MOTIVATE:
How are your intentions progressing
- are any adjustments necessary?

MOOD:

1st Quarter Moon: Motivate. Renew momentum.
Identify challenges. Reevaluate. Set boundaries. Adjust.

TRACKING:

☆

TOP TASKS:
☐
☐
☐

DAILY GRATITUDE:

6	2
7	3
8	4
9	5
10	6
11	7
12	8
1	9

GIBBOUS MOON, WAXING / EXPAND:
What can you do to
re-motivate yourself?

MOOD:

Gibbous Moon: Expand. Improve. Recognize luck. Connect.
Notice synchronicities. Tend to health. Listen to self.

TRACKING:

TOP TASKS:

☐
☐
☐

DAILY GRATITUDE:

6		2	
7		3	
8		4	
9		5	
10		6	
11		7	
12		8	
1		9	

GIBBOUS MOON, WAXING / EXPAND:

What is something
giving you hope right now?

MOOD:

TRACKING:

☆

TOP TASKS:
- [ ]
- [ ]
- [ ]

DAILY GRATITUDE:

6	2
7	3
8	4
9	5
10	6
11	7
12	8
1	9

GIBBOUS MOON, WAXING / EXPAND:
What is something
you're looking forward to?

MOOD:

FEB.01,'23

♊ ♋

TRACKING:

☆

TOP TASKS:
☐
☐
☐

DAILY GRATITUDE:

6		2	
7		3	
8		4	
9		5	
10		6	
11		7	
12		8	
1		9	

GIBBOUS MOON, WAXING / EXPAND:
Where could you be
saving money or resources?

MOOD:

FEB.02,'23

TRACKING:

☆

TOP TASKS:
☐
☐
☐

DAILY GRATITUDE:

6	2
7	3
8	4
9	5
10	6
11	7
12	8
1	9

GIBBOUS MOON, WAXING / EXPAND:
How could you be
communicating better?

MOOD:

FEB.03,'23
FRIDAY | WEEK 5

TRACKING:

TOP TASKS:
- [ ]
- [ ]
- [ ]

DAILY GRATITUDE:

6	2
7	3
8	4
9	5
10	6
11	7
12	8
1	9

GIBBOUS MOON, WAXING / EXPAND:
In what ways can you practice self-love today?

MOOD:

FEB.04,'23

SATURDAY | WEEK 5

♋ ♌

TRACKING:

TOP TASKS:

☐
☐
☐

DAILY GRATITUDE:

6	2
7	3
8	4
9	5
10	6
11	7
12	8
1	9

GIBBOUS MOON, WAXING / EXPAND:

Who could give you
some valuable feedback?

MOOD:

LEO FULL MOON

"SNOW MOON" | FEBRUARY 05, 2023

The February Full Moon appears in the loyal sign of Leo.

Leo is all about creativity, charisma, bravery, generosity, theatrics, romance + expressions of joy. This Full Moon encourages us to have fun + celebrate all of life.

Opposite the Full Moon is the Sun in Aquarius, which is all about idealism, innovation + independence. Therefore, the Leo-Aquarius Sun-Moon duality challenges us to balance our expressions of attachment vs. detachment.

Leo likes the spotlight but Aquarius knows how to work with an ensemble. Take time to evaluate where you fall on this spectrum and which roles you play on the stage of life. This Full Moon may also confront our feelings around feedback – both how we give it + how we receive it. Fear of criticism is normal – but worse when you have a tough inner critic. Summon courage to push through self-doubt + insecurity.

Anxieties could run a little high due to the Full Moon squaring Uranus/Taurus (chaos). Proceed with caution. Leo energy thrives with a healthy ego but unpredictability risks vulnerability + concern – we may feel edgy or capricious. Resist temptation to paint the room black even though the potential for a big, bad mood is palpable. Avoid getting swept away by practicing gratitude + taking time to meditate.

This Leo Full Moon is perfect for living life to it's fullest – you don't need validation from anyone for anything. Celebrate + forgive all parts of yourself.

Set the mood (page 12), then take time to respond to the Full Moon worksheet on the following pages.

How do you both give and react to feedback and criticism?

How would you describe your attachment style?

Where are you feeling most vulnerable right now?

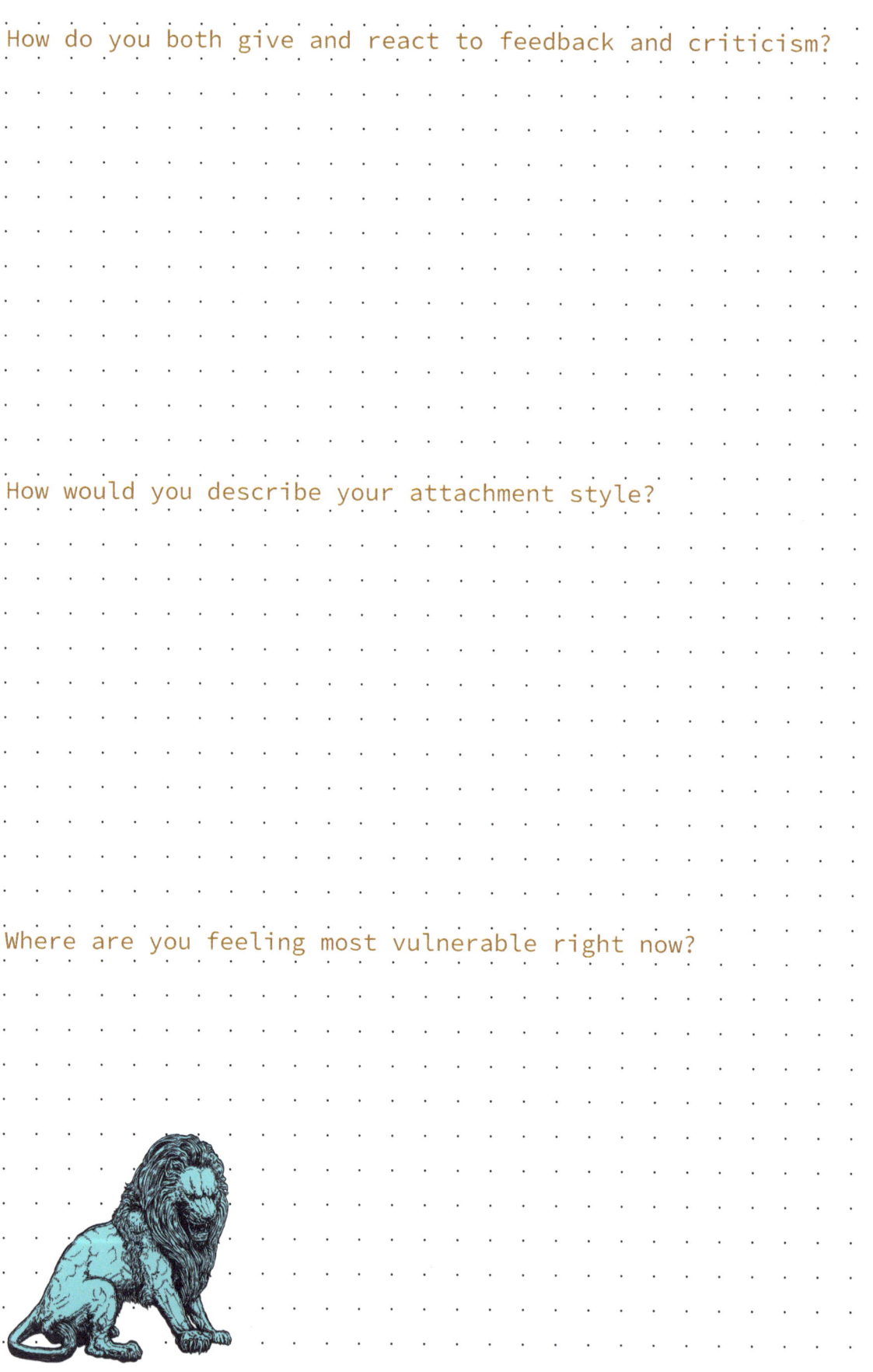

Describe your favorite form of creative self-expression:

Revisit your intentions from the last New Moon – what progress have you made? What worked, what didn't?

What are you releasing this Full Moon and why?

FEB.05,'23

SUNDAY | WEEK 5

♌

☆

TOP TASKS:
☐
☐
☐

DAILY GRATITUDE:

6 ....
7 ....
8 ....
9 ....
10 ....
11 ....
12 ....
1 ....

2 ....
3 ....
4 ....
5 ....
6 ....
7 ....
8 ....
9 ....

FULL MOON, HARVEST (LA, NY, LON):
Take time to complete the Full Moon
worksheet on previous pages!

MOOD:

Full Moon: Enjoy. Harvest. Heal. Bloom. Have fun.
Get creative. Celebrate progress. Acknowledge growth.

FEB.06,'23

MONDAY | WEEK 6

◯ ♌ ♍

TRACKING:

☆

TOP TASKS:
- ☐
- ☐
- ☐

DAILY GRATITUDE:

6	2
7	3
8	4
9	5
10	6
11	7
12	8
1	9

FULL MOON, HARVEST (SYD):

Celebrate!

MOOD:

FEB.07,'23

TUESDAY | WEEK 6

◯ ♍

TRACKING:

☆

TOP TASKS:

☐
☐
☐

DAILY GRATITUDE:

6		2	
7		3	
8		4	
9		5	
10		6	
11		7	
12		8	
1		9	

DISSEMINATING MOON, WANING / REFLECT:

Describe a recent situation
that you feel you handled well.

MOOD:

Disseminating Moon: Reflect. Be appreciative. Share Wisdom.
Educate. Reveal. Process. Review boundaries. Write + record.

🌑 ♍

TRACKING:

☆

TOP TASKS:
- ☐
- ☐
- ☐

DAILY GRATITUDE:

6		2	
7		3	
8		4	
9		5	
10		6	
11		7	
12		8	
1		9	

DISSEMINATING MOON. WANING / REFLECT:
What is something you've
started that needs to be finished?

MOOD:

TRACKING:

☆

TOP TASKS:
☐
☐
☐

DAILY GRATITUDE:

6		2	
7		3	
8		4	
9		5	
10		6	
11		7	
12		8	
1		9	

DISSEMINATING MOON, WANING / REFLECT:

Breakdown something stopping you
which requires deeper analysis.

MOOD:

♎

TRACKING:

☆

TOP TASKS:

- [ ]
- [ ]
- [ ]

DAILY GRATITUDE:

6	2
7	3
8	4
9	5
10	6
11	7
12	8
1	9

DISSEMINATING MOON. WANING / REFLECT:

How can you share something
beneficial with your community?

MOOD:

♎ ♏

TRACKING:

TOP TASKS:
☐
☐
☐

DAILY GRATITUDE:

6		2	
7		3	
8		4	
9		5	
10		6	
11		7	
12		8	
1		9	

DISSEMINATING MOON, WANING / REFLECT:
Which relationships have
you counted on lately?

MOOD:

MERCURY → AQUARIUS

♏

☆

TOP TASKS:

☐

☐

☐

DAILY GRATITUDE:

6		2
7		3
8		4
9		5
10		6
11		7
12		8
1		9

DISSEMINATING MOON. WANING / REFLECT:

What is making you feel doubt or
fear and how can you change it?

MOOD:

TRACKING:

TOP TASKS:
- [ ]
- [ ]
- [ ]

DAILY GRATITUDE:

6		2	
7		3	
8		4	
9		5	
10		6	
11		7	
12		8	
1		9	

LAST QUARTER MOON, RELEASE:

What can you forgive and let go of?

MOOD:

Last Quarter Moon: Release. Clear the air. Forgive. Surrender. Embrace calm. Find balance. Clear path.

FEB.14,'23

TUESDAY | WEEK 7

♏ ↗

☆

TOP TASKS:
- ☐
- ☐
- ☐

DAILY GRATITUDE:

6	2
7	3
8	4
9	5
10	6
11	7
12	8
1	9

BALSAMIC MOON, WANING / RESTORE:

What recent wins
are you happy about?

MOOD:

Balsamic Moon: Restore. Trust intuition. Rest. Dream.
Examine ego. Find grace. Clean + declutter. Self-care.

FEB.15,'23
WEDNESDAY | WEEK 7

TRACKING:

☆

TOP TASKS:
- [ ]
- [ ]
- [ ]

DAILY GRATITUDE:

6	2
7	3
8	4
9	5
10	6
11	7
12	8
1	9

BALSAMIC MOON, WANING / RESTORE:
Is there anything
you want to quit?

MOOD:

FEB.16,'23
THURSDAY | WEEK 7

TRACKING:

☆

TOP TASKS:
- ☐
- ☐
- ☐

DAILY GRATITUDE:

6 ....
7 ....
8 ....
9 ....
10 ....
11 ....
12 ....
1 ....

2 ....
3 ....
4 ....
5 ....
6 ....
7 ....
8 ....
9 ....

BALSAMIC MOON, WANING / RESTORE:
What is a piece of advice
you want to give yourself?

MOOD:

FEB.17,'23

FRIDAY | WEEK 7

♑

☆

TOP TASKS:
- [ ]
- [ ]
- [ ]

DAILY GRATITUDE:

6	2
7	3
8	4
9	5
10	6
11	7
12	8
1	9

BALSAMIC MOON, RESTORE / WANING:

What can you do to connect
deeper with your spiritual side?

MOOD:

FEB.18,'23

SATURDAY | WEEK 7

♑ ≈

☆

TOP TASKS:
- [ ]
- [ ]
- [ ]

DAILY GRATITUDE:

6 ....
7 ....
8 ....
9 ....
10 ....
11 ....
12 ....
1 ....

2 ....
3 ....
4 ....
5 ....
6 ....
7 ....
8 ....
9 ....

BALSAMIC MOON, RESTORE / WANING:

What can you do to relax today?

MOOD:

SUN → PISCES

PISCES SUPER NEW MOON

FEBRUARY 20, 2023

The February New Moon is in the psychic sign of Pisces.
Depending on your time zone this Moon may occur on 02.19.

Also a Supermoon, this New Moon is 3x more powerful than a
regular New Moon; perfect for tapping into our subconscious
and trusting our innermost voice.

Pisces is all about imagination, intuition, self-care,
empathy, emotional awareness + the unconscious. This New Moon
encourages us to take our dreams and make them reality. If
you can remember your dreams when you wake up, write them
down right away. Centering on powerful new beginnings, this
is a great time to visualize your desires from start to
finish — the more imaginative you can be, the better.

Saturn (discipline) is edging on Pisces for the 1st time
since 1996, preparing for his ~2.5 year tour starting 03.07.
The move from Aquarius to Pisces asks us to take greater
responsibility for the mind-numbing escapism of technology +
social media. Saturn is the planet of karma + rules, so his
stay in Pisces highlights our ideas of fantasy vs. reality.
We will need to confront our addictions + worst temptations.
Consider setting screen time limits on all of your devices.

A powerful Super New Moon such as this gives us permission
to be extra esoteric while indulging in excessive self-care.
Some suggestions: read tarot cards, cleanse crystals, apply a
face mask, take a bath, journal + get full night's rest.
You deserve it.

Set the mood (page 12), then take time to respond
to the New Moon worksheet on the following pages.

Visualize your dreams — write, draw, etc.
The more imaginative, the better:

In what ways can you practice self-care during this New Moon?

Write down some goals you'd like to work on this Lunar Cycle:

Write out a clear intention for this New Moon:

≋

TRACKING:

☆

TOP TASKS:

☐
☐
☐

DAILY GRATITUDE:

6 ....
7 ....
8 ....
9 ....
10 ....
11 ....
12 ....
1 ....

2 ....
3 ....
4 ....
5 ....
6 ....
7 ....
8 ....
9 ....

SUPER NEW MOON, MANIFEST (LA):
Consider your intentions and
create space for a New Moon Ritual.

MOOD:

♒ ♓

TRACKING:

☆

TOP TASKS:
- [ ]
- [ ]
- [ ]

DAILY GRATITUDE:

6	2
7	3
8	4
9	5
10	6
11	7
12	8
1	9

SUPER NEW MOON, MANIFEST (NY, LON, SYD)**:** Take time to complete the New Moon worksheet on previous pages.

MOOD:

VENUS → ARIES

New Moon: Manifest. Set intentions. Plant Seeds.
Follow heart. Identify goals + dreams for the new cycle.

♓

TRACKING:

☆

TOP TASKS:
- ☐
- ☐
- ☐

DAILY GRATITUDE:

6		2	
7		3	
8		4	
9		5	
10		6	
11		7	
12		8	
1		9	

CRESCENT MOON, PROGRESS / WAXING:

What is 1 small action you can take today to kick off your intentions?

MOOD:

Crescent Moon: Progress. Take Action. Trust instincts.
Make plans. Be courageous. Build good habits. Innovate.

♓ ♈

TRACKING:

TOP TASKS:
- ☐
- ☐
- ☐

DAILY GRATITUDE:

6 ....
7 ....
8 ....
9 ....
10 ....
11 ....
12 ....
1 ....

2 ....
3 ....
4 ....
5 ....
6 ....
7 ....
8 ....
9 ....

CRESCENT MOON, WAXING / PROGRESS:

Which of your strengths
can help you right now?

MOOD:

♈

☆

TOP TASKS:

☐
☐
☐

DAILY GRATITUDE:

6

7

8

9

10

11

12

1

2

3

4

5

6

7

8

9

CRESCENT MOON, WAXING / PROGRESS:
What's distracting you
and how can you change it?

MOOD:

FEB.24,'23
FRIDAY | WEEK 8

♈ ♉

☆

TOP TASKS:
- ☐
- ☐
- ☐

DAILY GRATITUDE:

6	2
7	3
8	4
9	5
10	6
11	7
12	8
1	9

CRESCENT MOON, WAXING / PROGRESS:
What kind of research can
you do to support your intentions?

MOOD:

TRACKING:

☆

TOP TASKS:

☐

☐

☐

DAILY GRATITUDE:

6

7

8

9

10

11

12

1

2

3

4

5

6

7

8

9

CRESCENT MOON, WAXING / PROGRESS:

How can you improve
your morning routine?

MOOD:

TRACKING:

TOP TASKS:
☐
☐
☐

DAILY GRATITUDE:

6		2	
7		3	
8		4	
9		5	
10		6	
11		7	
12		8	
1		9	

CRESCENT MOON, WAXING / PROGRESS:

How can you improve
your evening routine?

MOOD:

TRACKING:

☆

TOP TΔSKS:

☐
☐
☐

DΔILY GRΔTITUDE:

6	2
7	3
8	4
9	5
10	6
11	7
12	8
1	9

1ST QUΔRTER MOON, MOTIVΔTE:

How are your intentions progressing — are any adjustments necessary?

MOOD:

1st Quarter Moon: Motivate. Renew momentum. Identify challenges. Reevaluate. Set boundaries. Adjust.

FEB.28,'23

TUESDAY | WEEK 9

TRACKING:

☆

TOP TASKS:

☐
☐
☐

DAILY GRATITUDE:

6		2	
7		3	
8		4	
9		5	
10		6	
11		7	
12		8	
1		9	

GIBBOUS MOON, WAXING / EXPAND:

What can you do to
re-motivate yourself?

MOOD:

Gibbous Moon: Expand. Improve. Recognize luck. Connect.
Notice synchronicities. Tend to health. Listen to self.

MAR.01,'23
WEDNESDAY | WEEK 9

♊ ♋

TRACKING:

☆

TOP TASKS:
- ☐
- ☐
- ☐

DAILY GRATITUDE:

6	2	
7	3	
8	4	
9	5	
10	6	
11	7	
12	8	
1	9	

GIBBOUS MOON, WAXING / EXPAND:
What is something
giving you hope right now?

MOOD:

TRACKING:

TOP TASKS:
- [ ]
- [ ]
- [ ]

DAILY GRATITUDE:

6		2	
7		3	
8		4	
9		5	
10		6	
11		7	
12		8	
1		9	

GIBBOUS MOON, WAXING / EXPAND:
What is something
you're looking forward to?

MOOD:

MERCURY → PISCES

♋ ♌

TRACKING:

☆

TOP TASKS:
- ☐
- ☐
- ☐

DAILY GRATITUDE:

6		2	
7		3	
8		4	
9		5	
10		6	
11		7	
12		8	
1		9	

GIBBOUS MOON, WAXING / EXPAND:
Where could you be
saving money or resources?

MOOD:

TRACKING:

♌

TOP TASKS:
- [ ]
- [ ]
- [ ]

DAILY GRATITUDE:

6		2	
7		3	
8		4	
9		5	
10		6	
11		7	
12		8	
1		9	

GIBBOUS MOON, WAXING / EXPAND:

How can you be communicating better?

MOOD:

♌ ♍

TRACKING:

☆

TOP TASKS:
- ☐
- ☐
- ☐

DAILY GRATITUDE:

6	2
7	3
8	4
9	5
10	6
11	7
12	8
1	9

GIBBOUS MOON, WAXING / EXPAND:

In what ways can you
practice self-love today?

MOOD:

TRACKING:

TOP TASKS:

☐

☐

☐

DAILY GRATITUDE:

6		2
7		3
8		4
9		5
10		6
11		7
12		8
1		9

GIBBOUS MOON, WAXING / EXPAND:

Who could give you

some valuable feedback?

MOOD:

VIRGO FULL MOON

"WORM MOON" | MARCH 07, 2023

The March Full Moon appears in the dutiful sign of Virgo.

Virgo is all about effort, precision, intelligence, analysis efficiency + attention to detail. This Full Moon encourages us to do some spring cleaning + update our routines.

Opposite the Full Moon is the Sun in Pisces, which is all about empathy, spirituality + flights of fancy. Therefore, the Virgo-Pisces Sun-Moon polarity challenges us to balance our need for control vs. the art of letting go.

Virgo's diligent nature thrives within structure, whereas Pisces takes inspiration from chaos. Take time to evaluate where you fall on this spectrum. This Full Moon also emphasizes how your physical health + mental health both impact your overall health. This is a supportive time for making appointments with doctors and researching healthier alternatives for your lifestyle.

Today, Saturn (discipline) shifts out of Aquarius and into Pisces for it's 1st visit in ~30 years. Saturn is all about growing up + taking accountability, serving as the authority of karma + justice. Stationed in Aquarius, Saturn tested our individual impact on community (pandemic) and our greater responsibilities as global citizens (Online movements, protests). As Saturn moves into Pisces, he highlights our issues with fantasy vs. reality. Because Pisces is the last sign of the zodiac, Saturn's ultimate test combines lessons derived from all other astrological signs. Keep in mind: hard lessons often make for the best art.

Set the mood (page 12), then take time to respond to the Full Moon worksheet on the following pages.

Consider Saturn's visit to Aquarius over the last 2 1/2 years: what did you learn as an individual engaging with community?

How can you better balance control vs. the art of letting go?

Which routines are working for you and how can you improve?

What ways can you can improve your mental + physical health?

Revisit your intentions from the last New Moon –
what progress have you made? What worked, what didn't?

What are you releasing this Full Moon and why?

○   ♍

☆

TOP TASKS:
☐
☐
☐

DAILY GRATITUDE:

6		2
7		3
8		4
9		5
10		6
11		7
12		8
1		9

FULL WORM MOON, HARVEST (LA, NY, LON, SYD): Take time to complete the Full Moon worksheet on previous pages.

MOOD:

SATURN → PISCES

Full Moon: Enjoy. Harvest. Heal. Bloom. Have fun. Get creative. Celebrate progress. Acknowledge growth.

♍ ♎

TRACKING:

TOP TASKS:
- ☐
- ☐
- ☐

DAILY GRATITUDE:

6		2	
7		3	
8		4	
9		5	
10		6	
11		7	
12		8	
1		9	

DISSEMINATING MOON, REFLECT / WANING:
Review your boundaries — what healthy adjustments can you make?

MOOD:

Disseminating Moon: Reflect. Be appreciative. Share Wisdom. Educate. Reveal. Process. Review boundaries. Write + record.

MAR.09,'23

♎

TRACKING:

☆

TOP TASKS:
- ☐
- ☐
- ☐

DAILY GRATITUDE:

6	2	
7	3	
8	4	
9	5	
10	6	
11	7	
12	8	
1	9	

DISSEMINATING MOON, REFLECT / WANING:
Describe a recent situation
that you feel you handled well.

MOOD:

☾ ♎

TRACKING:

☆

TOP TASKS:
- ☐
- ☐
- ☐

DAILY GRATITUDE:

6	2
7	3
8	4
9	5
10	6
11	7
12	8
1	9

DISSEMINATING MOON, REFLECT / WANING:
What is something you started
that needs to be finished?

MOOD:

MAR.11,'23

♎ ♏

TRACKING:

☆

TOP TASKS:
- [ ]
- [ ]
- [ ]

DAILY GRATITUDE:

6		2	
7		3	
8		4	
9		5	
10		6	
11		7	
12		8	
1		9	

DISSEMINATING MOON, REFLECT / WANING:
Breakdown something stopping
you which requires deeper analysis.

MOOD:

MAR.12,'23

SUNDAY | WEEK 12

♏

TRACKING:

☆

TOP TASKS:
- ☐
- ☐
- ☐

DAILY GRATITUDE:

6	2	
7	3	
8	4	
9	5	
10	6	
11	7	
12	8	
1	9	

DISSEMINATING MOON, REFLECT / WANING:
How can you share something
beneficial with your community?

MOOD:

JUPITER ♥ CHIRON

TRACKING:

TOP TASKS:

☐
☐
☐

DAILY GRATITUDE:

6 ....
7 ....
8 ....
9 ....
10 ....
11 ....
12 ....
1 ....

2 ....
3 ....
4 ....
5 ....
6 ....
7 ....
8 ....
9 ....

DISSEMINATING MOON, REFLECT / WANING:

Which relationships have
you counted on lately?

MOOD:

TRACKING:

TOP TASKS:
- [ ]
- [ ]
- [ ]

DAILY GRATITUDE:

6	2
7	3
8	4
9	5
10	6
11	7
12	8
1	9

DISSEMINATING MOON, WANING / REFLECT:
What is making you feel doubt
or fear and how can you change it?

MOOD:

↗ ♑

☆

TOP TASKS:
☐
☐
☐

DAILY GRATITUDE:

6	2
7	3
8	4
9	5
10	6
11	7
12	8
1	9

LAST QUARTER MOON, RELEASE:

What can you forgive and let go of?

MOOD:

Last Quarter Moon: Release. Clear the air. Forgive.
Surrender. Embrace calm. Find balance. Clear path.

MAR.16,'23

♑

☆

TOP TASKS:

☐
☐
☐

DAILY GRATITUDE:

6 ....
7 ....
8 ....
9 ....
10 ....
11 ....
12 ....
1 ....

2 ....
3 ....
4 ....
5 ....
6 ....
7 ....
8 ....
9 ....

BALSAMIC MOON, RESTORE / WANING:

What recent wins
are you happy about?

MOOD:

VENUS → TAURUS

Balsamic Moon: Restore. Trust intuition. Rest. Dream.
Examine ego. Find grace. Clean + declutter. Self-care.

♑ ♒

TRACKING:

☆

TOP TASKS:

☐

☐

☐

DAILY GRATITUDE:

6		2	
7		3	
8		4	
9		5	
10		6	
11		7	
12		8	
1		9	

BALSAMIC MOON, RESTORE / WANING:

Is there anything
you want to quit?

MOOD:

MAR.18,'23

SATURDAY | WEEK 11

TOP TASKS:

- [ ]
- [ ]
- [ ]

DAILY GRATITUDE:

6	2
7	3
8	4
9	5
10	6
11	7
12	8
1	9

BALSAMIC MOON, RESTORE / WANING:

What is a piece of advice
you want to give yourself?

MOOD:

MAR.19,'23

SUNDAY | WEEK 11

≋ ♓

☆

TOP TASKS:
- ☐
- ☐
- ☐

DAILY GRATITUDE:

6		2	
7		3	
8		4	
9		5	
10		6	
11		7	
12		8	
1		9	

BALSAMIC MOON, RESTORE / WANING:

What can you do to connect deeper with your spiritual side?

MOOD:

MERCURY → ARIES

MAR.20,'23
MONDAY | WEEK 12

♓

☆

TOP TASKS:
- ☐
- ☐
- ☐

DAILY GRATITUDE:

6		2	
7		3	
8		4	
9		5	
10		6	
11		7	
12		8	
1		9	

BALSAMIC MOON, RESTORE / WANING:
Which habits can you continue
(or begin) this next Lunar Cycle?

MOOD:

SUN → ARIES

N. HEMISPHERE SPRING EQUINOX
S. HEMISPHERE FALL EQUINOX

ARIES NEW MOON

MARCH 21, 2023

The March New Moon occurs in the confident sign of Aries.
Kicking off the Astrological New Year + the Spring Equinox,
this is (yet again) the perfect time for new beginnings.

Aries is all about motivation, leadership, passion, ego,
self-determination + quick decisions. This New Moon suggests
that we follow our impulses + trust our 1st reactions. Aries
conjures excitement, and a certain amount of moxie, so this
a great time to get your way. Assertiveness may haphazardly
turn abrasive if you don't have a plan for your actions.

Pluto (power) is moving into Aquarius this week after being
in Capricorn since 2008. He'll bounce back + forth between
Capricorn + Aquarius before settling in for his ~20 year stay
in late 2024. Because his orbit takes ~248 years, we will not
experience his return in our lifetimes.

Pluto signifies endings, awakenings + rebirths by
dramatically transforming everything in his path. During
his journey through patriarchal Capricorn, Pluto wrecked
havoc on our societal structures, financial organizations +
ideas of governance. From the stock market to social justice,
there is no better example of this than the United States -
which is at the end of it's own "Pluto Return" and
experiencing a rage against the machine on multiple levels.

As Pluto moves into Aquarius, democracy will continue to be
tested as we confront power dynamics in our politics,
communities, friendships + scientific advancements. We will
be asked to pursue progressiveness while avoiding
self-righteousness. Don't start a war in your circles.

Set the mood (page 12), then take time to respond
to the New Moon worksheet on the following pages.

In what ways can you be advocating better for yourself?

Where do you notice self-righteousness in yourself + others?

Release your guilts, shames and fears by naming them now:

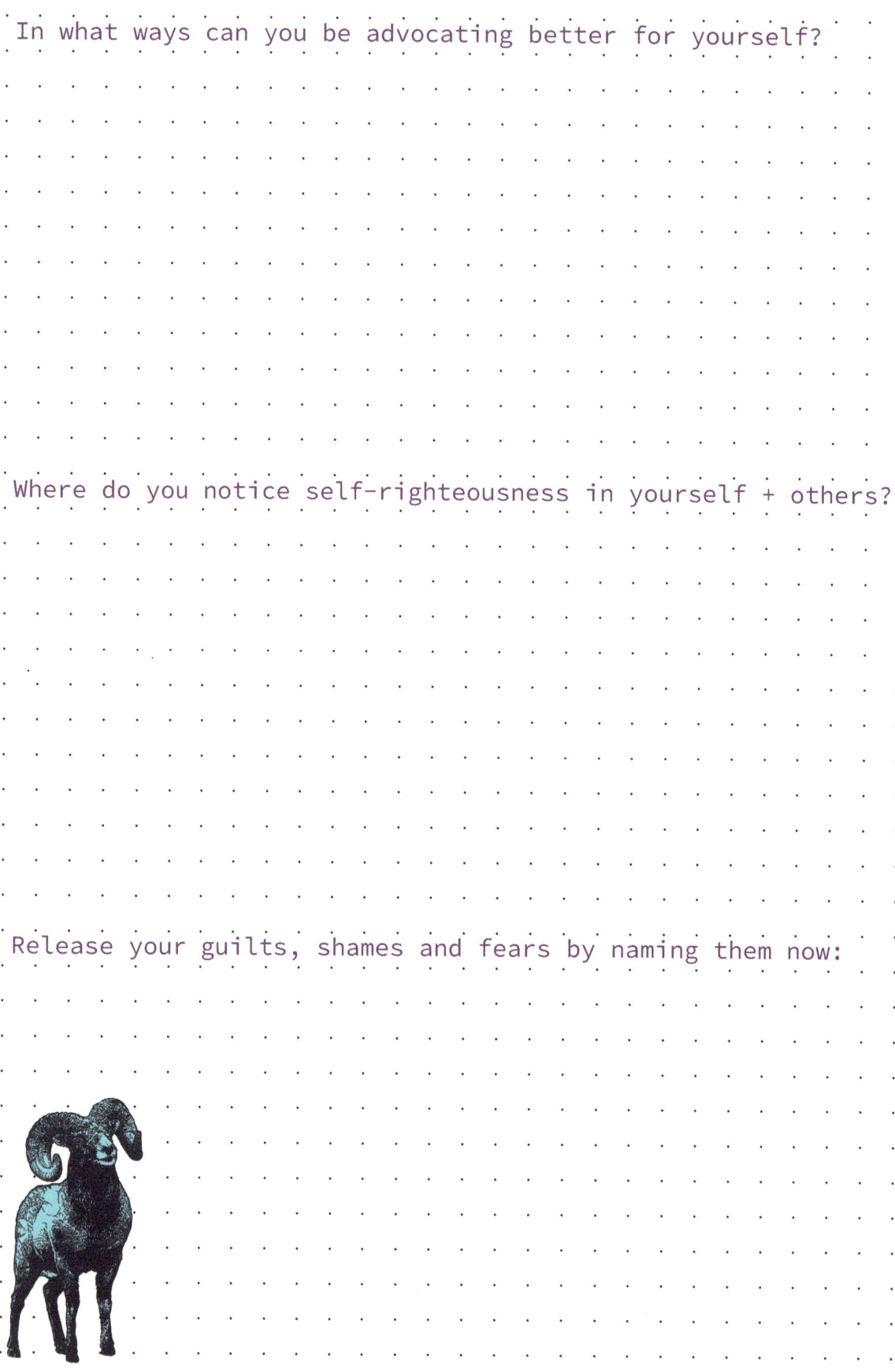

What do you believe is worth fighting for?

Write down some goals you'd like to work on this Lunar Cycle:

Write out a clear intention for this New Moon:

⊗ ♓ ♈

☆

TOP TASKS:
☐
☐
☐

DAILY GRATITUDE:

6	2
7	3
8	4
9	5
10	6
11	7
12	8
1	9

NEW MOON, MANIFEST (LA, NY, LON):
Take time to complete the New Moon
worksheet on the previous pages.

MOOD:

New Moon: Manifest. Set intentions. Plant Seeds.
Follow heart. Identify goals + dreams for the new cycle.

MAR.22,'23

♈

TRACKING:

☆

TOP TASKS:
- ☐
- ☐
- ☐

DAILY GRATITUDE:

6

7

8

9

10

11

12

1

2

3

4

5

6

7

8

9

NEW MOON, MANIFEST (SYD):

Meditate on your new or
revived intentions today.

MOOD:

THURSDAY | WEEK 12

♈ ♉

TRACKING:

☆

TOP TASKS:
- ☐
- ☐
- ☐

DAILY GRATITUDE:

6	2
7	3
8	4
9	5
10	6
11	7
12	8
1	9

CRESCENT MOON, PROGRESS / WAXING:

What is one 1 action you can take today to kick off your intentions?

MOOD:

PLUTO → AQUARIUS

Crescent Moon: Progress. Take Action. Trust instincts.
Make plans. Be courageous. Build good habits. Innovate.

MAR.24,'23
FRIDAY | WEEK 12

♉

TRACKING:

☆

TOP TASKS:
☐
☐
☐

DAILY GRATITUDE:

6 ....
7 ....
8 ....
9 ....
10 ....
11 ....
12 ....
1 ....

2 ....
3 ....
4 ....
5 ....
6 ....
7 ....
8 ....
9 ....

CRESCENT MOON, PROGRESS / WAXING:
Which of your strengths
can help you now?

MOOD:

♉

TRACKING:

☆

TOP TASKS:
- ☐
- ☐
- ☐

DAILY GRATITUDE:

6		2	
7		3	
8		4	
9		5	
10		6	
11		7	
12		8	
1		9	

CRESCENT MOON, PROGRESS / WAXING:

What's distracting you
and how can you change it?

MOOD:

MARS → CANCER

MAR.26,'23

♉ ♊

TRACKING:

☆

TOP TASKS:

- ☐
- ☐
- ☐

DAILY GRATITUDE:

6		2	
7		3	
8		4	
9		5	
10		6	
11		7	
12		8	
1		9	

CRESCENT MOON, WAXING / PROGRESS:

What kind of research can you
do to support your intentions?

MOOD:

Ⅱ

TRACKING:

TOP TASKS:
- [ ]
- [ ]
- [ ]

DAILY GRATITUDE:

6		2	
7		3	
8		4	
9		5	
10		6	
11		7	
12		8	
1		9	

CRESCENT MOON, PROGRESS / WAXING:

How can you improve
your morning routine?

MOOD:

MAR.28,'23

♊ ♋

TRACKING:

☆

TOP TASKS:
- ☐
- ☐
- ☐

DAILY GRATITUDE:

6 ....

7 ....

8 ....

9 ....

10 ....

11 ....

12 ....

1 ....

2 ....

3 ....

4 ....

5 ....

6 ....

7 ....

8 ....

9 ....

CRESCENT MOON, PROGRESS / WAXING:

How can you improve
your evening routine?

MOOD:

WEDNESDAY | WEEK 13

TRACKING:

TOP TASKS:
- [ ]
- [ ]
- [ ]

DAILY GRATITUDE:

6
7
8
9
10
11
12
1

2
3
4
5
6
7
8
9

1ST QUARTER MOON, MOTIVATE:
How are your intentions progressing – are any adjustments necessary?

MOOD:

1st Quarter Moon: Motivate. Renew momentum. Identify challenges. Reevaluate. Set boundaries. Adjust.

MAR.30,'23

TRACKING:

☆

TOP TASKS:
- ☐
- ☐
- ☐

DAILY GRATITUDE:

6	2
7	3
8	4
9	5
10	6
11	7
12	8
1	9

GIBBOUS MOON, EXPAND / WAXING:
What is something
giving you hope right now?

MOOD:

Gibbous Moon: Expand. Improve. Recognize luck. Connect.
Notice synchronicities. Tend to health. Listen to self.

TRACKING:

☆

TOP TASKS:

☐

☐

☐

DAILY GRATITUDE:

6		2	
7		3	
8		4	
9		5	
10		6	
11		7	
12		8	
1		9	

GIBBOUS MOON, EXPAND / WAXING:

What is something
you're looking forward to?

MOOD:

STATE-OF-SELF 3-MONTH CHECK-IN

Revisit page 20 to compare, track + acknowledge your growth. Based on the Astrological Houses, rate each area of life 1-10 and make notes in the space provided. Identify areas which deserve attention, improvement + appreciation.

How do I feel about myself?　　　　1 2 3 4 5 6 7 8 9 10

_____

_____

_____

How stable is my life?　　　　1 2 3 4 5 6 7 8 9 10

_____

_____

_____

How is my communication?　　　　1 2 3 4 5 6 7 8 9 10

_____

_____

_____

How is my home life?　　　　1 2 3 4 5 6 7 8 9 10

_____

_____

_____

How much am I enjoying myself?　　　　1 2 3 4 5 6 7 8 9 10

_____

_____

_____

How is my physical health?　　　　1 2 3 4 5 6 7 8 9 10

_____

_____

_____

How are my relationships?   1 2 3 4 5 6 7 8 9 10

How am I coping with change?   1 2 3 4 5 6 7 8 9 10

How much am I learning?   1 2 3 4 5 6 7 8 9 10

How is my reputation / career?   1 2 3 4 5 6 7 8 9 10

How are my friendships / community?   1 2 3 4 5 6 7 8 9 10

How is my sleep / self-care?   1 2 3 4 5 6 7 8 9 10

Areas of Attention and Appreciation Over Next 3 Months:

TRACKING:

☆

TOP TASKS:

☐

☐

☐

DAILY GRATITUDE:

6	2
7	3
8	4
9	5
10	6
11	7
12	8
1	9

GIBBOUS MOON, EXPAND / WAXING:

Where could you be

saving money or resources?

MOOD:

APR.02,'23
SUNDAY | WEEK 13

🌒 ♌ ♍

☆

TOP TASKS:
- ☐
- ☐
- ☐

DAILY GRATITUDE:

6	2
7	3
8	4
9	5
10	6
11	7
12	8
1	9

GIBBOUS MOON, EXPAND / WAXING:

How can you be
communicating better?

MOOD:

♏

TRACKING:

☆

TOP TASKS:
- ☐
- ☐
- ☐

DAILY GRATITUDE:

6		2
7		3
8		4
9		5
10		6
11		7
12		8
1		9

GIBBOUS MOON, WAXING / EXPAND:

In what ways can you
practice self-love today?

MOOD:

MERCURY → TAURUS

♍ ♎

TRACKING:

☆

TOP TASKS:
☐
☐
☐

DAILY GRATITUDE:

6 ....
7 ....
8 ....
9 ....
10 ....
11 ....
12 ....
1 ....

2 ....
3 ....
4 ....
5 ....
6 ....
7 ....
8 ....
9 ....

GIBBOUS MOON, WAXING / EXPAND:

Who could give you
some valuable feedback?

MOOD:

LIBRA FULL MOON

"PINK MOON" | APRIL 06, 2023

The April Full Moon is in the harmonious sign of Libra.
Depending on your time zone this Moon may appear on 04.05.

Libra is all about relationship, balance, justice, kindness,
peace, self-indulgence + weighing out the options. This Full
Moon serves as a reminder to seek equality + fairness.

Opposite the Full Moon is the Sun in Aries, which is intense,
direct + egocentric. Therefore, the Aries-Libra Sun-Moon
polarity challenges us to balance our individuality vs.
our roles in relationship - a.k.a. "me" vs. "us".

Libra's equitable nature loves to listen, whereas Aries
demands to be heard. Take time to evaluate where you fall
on this spectrum. This Full Moon asks us to consider how we
treat people and how we are treated by others. Get curious
about temperament + dysregulation. Find ways to peacefully
honor your needs without denying those of your partners. Be
open to feedback in pursuit of establishing a safer space.

Highlighting our relationships is Jupiter (growth) and
Chiron (healing). This optimistic alignment, has huge
potential to bring significant healing to our core wounds.
Stay open to reconciliation + forgiveness. Take this
opportunity to review the weight of negativity on your life.
Be prepared to release trauma + drop grudges - make room for
personal regeneration.

However, because Jupiter in Aries is also opposing the Moon,
beware of over-excitement. Resist becoming aggressive +
wasteful by practicing prudence + restraint.

Set the mood (page 12), then take time to respond
to the Full Moon worksheet on the following pages.

Describe a harmonious relationship in your life:
who is it with and what makes it balanced?

What is something in your life that deserves more fairness?

Weigh out the options of a hard decision you need to make:

Describe an area of your life that needs healing:
what will it take and how can you play an active part?

Revisit your intentions from the last New Moon – what
progress have you made? What worked, what didn't?

What are you releasing this Full Moon and why?

APR.05,'23
WEDNESD∆Y | WEEK 14

○　♎

☆

TOP T∆SKS:
- ☐
- ☐
- ☐

D∆ILY GR∆TITUDE:

6	2
7	3
8	4
9	5
10	6
11	7
12	8
1	9

FULL MOON, H∆RVEST (L∆):
Meditate + Celebrate

MOOD:

○ ♎

TRACKING:

☆

TOP TASKS:
- ☐
- ☐
- ☐

DAILY GRATITUDE:

6	2
7	3
8	4
9	5
10	6
11	7
12	8
1	9

FULL MOON, HARVEST (NY, LON, SYD):
Take time to complete the Full Moon
worksheet on the previous pages.

MOOD:

Full Moon: Enjoy. Harvest. Heal. Bloom. Have fun.
Get creative. Celebrate progress. Acknowledge growth.

☾ ♎ ♏

TRACKING:

☆

TOP TASKS:
☐
☐
☐

DAILY GRATITUDE:

6
7
8
9
10
11
12
1

2
3
4
5
6
7
8
9

DISSEMINATING MOON, REFLECT / WANING:
Describe a recent situation
you feel that you handled well.

MOOD:

Disseminating Moon: Reflect. Be appreciative. Share Wisdom.
Educate. Reveal. Process. Review boundaries. Write + record.

TRACKING:

☆

TOP TASKS:
- [ ]
- [ ]
- [ ]

DAILY GRATITUDE:

6	2
7	3
8	4
9	5
10	6
11	7
12	8
1	9

DISSEMINATING MOON, REFLECT / WANING:
What is something you've started
that needs to be finished?

MOOD:

APR.09,'23
SUNDAY | WEEK 14

♏ ♐

☆

TOP TASKS:
- ☐
- ☐
- ☐

DAILY GRATITUDE:

6		2	
7		3	
8		4	
9		5	
10		6	
11		7	
12		8	
1		9	

DISSEMINATING MOON, REFLECT / WANING:
Breakdown something stopping you
which requires deeper analysis.

MOOD:

TRACKING:

☆

TOP TASKS:

☐
☐
☐

DAILY GRATITUDE:

6

7

8

9

10

11

12

1

2

3

4

5

6

7

8

9

DISSEMINATING MOON, REFLECT / WANING:

How can you share something
beneficial with your community?

MOOD:

TRACKING:

☆

TOP TASKS:

☐
☐
☐

DAILY GRATITUDE:

6		2	
7		3	
8		4	
9		5	
10		6	
11		7	
12		8	
1		9	

DISSEMINATING MOON, REFLECT / WANING:

Which relationships
have you counted on lately?

MOOD:

VENUS → GEMINI

TRACKING:

TOP TASKS:
- [ ]
- [ ]
- [ ]

DAILY GRATITUDE:

6	2
7	3
8	4
9	5
10	6
11	7
12	8
1	9

DISSEMINATING MOON, REFLECT / WANING:
What is making you feel doubt or fear and how can you change it?

MOOD:

♑ ♒

TRACKING:

☆

TOP TASKS:
- ☐
- ☐
- ☐

DAILY GRATITUDE:

6		2	
7		3	
8		4	
9		5	
10		6	
11		7	
12		8	
1		9	

LAST QUARTER MOON, RELEASE:
What can you forgive and let go of?

MOOD:

Last Quarter Moon: Release. Clear the air. Forgive.
Surrender. Embrace calm. Find balance. Clear path.

APR.14,'23

FRIDAY | WEEK 15

TOP TASKS:
- [ ]
- [ ]
- [ ]

DAILY GRATITUDE:

6	2
7	3
8	4
9	5
10	6
11	7
12	8
1	9

BALSAMIC MOON, RESTORE / WANING:

What recent wins
are you happy about?

MOOD:

Balsamic Moon: Restore. Trust intuition. Rest. Dream.
Examine ego. Find grace. Clean + declutter. Self-care.

APR.15,'23

SATURDAY | WEEK 15

≋ ♓

☆

TOP TASKS:
- ☐
- ☐
- ☐

DAILY GRATITUDE:

6	2
7	3
8	4
9	5
10	6
11	7
12	8
1	9

BALSAMIC MOON, RESTORE / WANING:
Is there anything
you want to quit?

MOOD:

APR.16,'23

SUNDAY | WEEK 15

⧖ ♓

☆

TOP TASKS:

☐
☐
☐

DAILY GRATITUDE:

6		2	
7		3	
8		4	
9		5	
10		6	
11		7	
12		8	
1		9	

BALSAMIC MOON, RESTORE / WANING:

What is a piece of advice
you want to give yourself?

MOOD:

♓

TRACKING:

☆

TOP TASKS:

☐
☐
☐

DAILY GRATITUDE:

6	2
7	3
8	4
9	5
10	6
11	7
12	8
1	9

BALSAMIC MOON, RESTORE / WANING:

What can you do to connect
deeper with your spiritual side?

MOOD:

♓ ♈

TRACKING:

☆

TOP TASKS:

- [ ]
- [ ]
- [ ]

DAILY GRATITUDE:

6	2
7	3
8	4
9	5
10	6
11	7
12	8
1	9

BALSAMIC MOON, RESTORE / WANING:

Which habits can you continue
(or begin) this next Lunar Cycle?

MOOD:

ARIES NEW MOON ECLIPSE

APRIL 20, 2023

The April New Moon is in the motivated sign of Aries.
Depending on your time zone this Moon may occur on 04.19.

A Solar Eclipse is 3x more powerful than a regular New Moon,
and is known to herald new beginnings + big changes. Not only
is this the 2nd New Moon in Aries in a row, but it's also
the 1st Eclipse in the Aries-Libra set (which will continue
through March 2025). Supercharged to the max, this New Moon
is also a Total Solar Eclipse (viewable in Australia).

Aries is all about leadership, passion, self-determination,
ego, drive + quick decisions. This New Moon encourages us to
follow gut impulses + stand up for ourselves. Over the next
~2 years, the Aries-Libra axis will challenge us to work on
our sense of individuality vs. our relationships - "me" vs.
"us". Take time to evaluate where you fall on this spectrum.

When the Moon's North Node (purpose/fate) is in Aries, we're
asked to review how we feel about ourselves. We're asked to
create a better self-relationship by having the audacity to
be our own best friend. Consider an update to personal style
+ outward appearances to be more aligned with who you've
become. Lean into your more ambitious plans, for anything you
start now has the potential to bring monumental developments
to your sense of self.

Squaring this Eclipse is Pluto (power), who will be dipping
back + forth between Aquarius + Capricorn until the end of
2024. A tense time for the world at large, expect more
foundational shifts in how we relate to ourselves and others
across the socio-political spectrum.

Set the mood (page 12), then take time to respond
to the New Moon worksheet on the following pages.

What is your current relationship like with yourself?

Where do you fall on the "me" vs. "us" spectrum of life?:

Review your style and outward appearance - does it vibe with
who you've become? What wardrobe updates could you embrace?

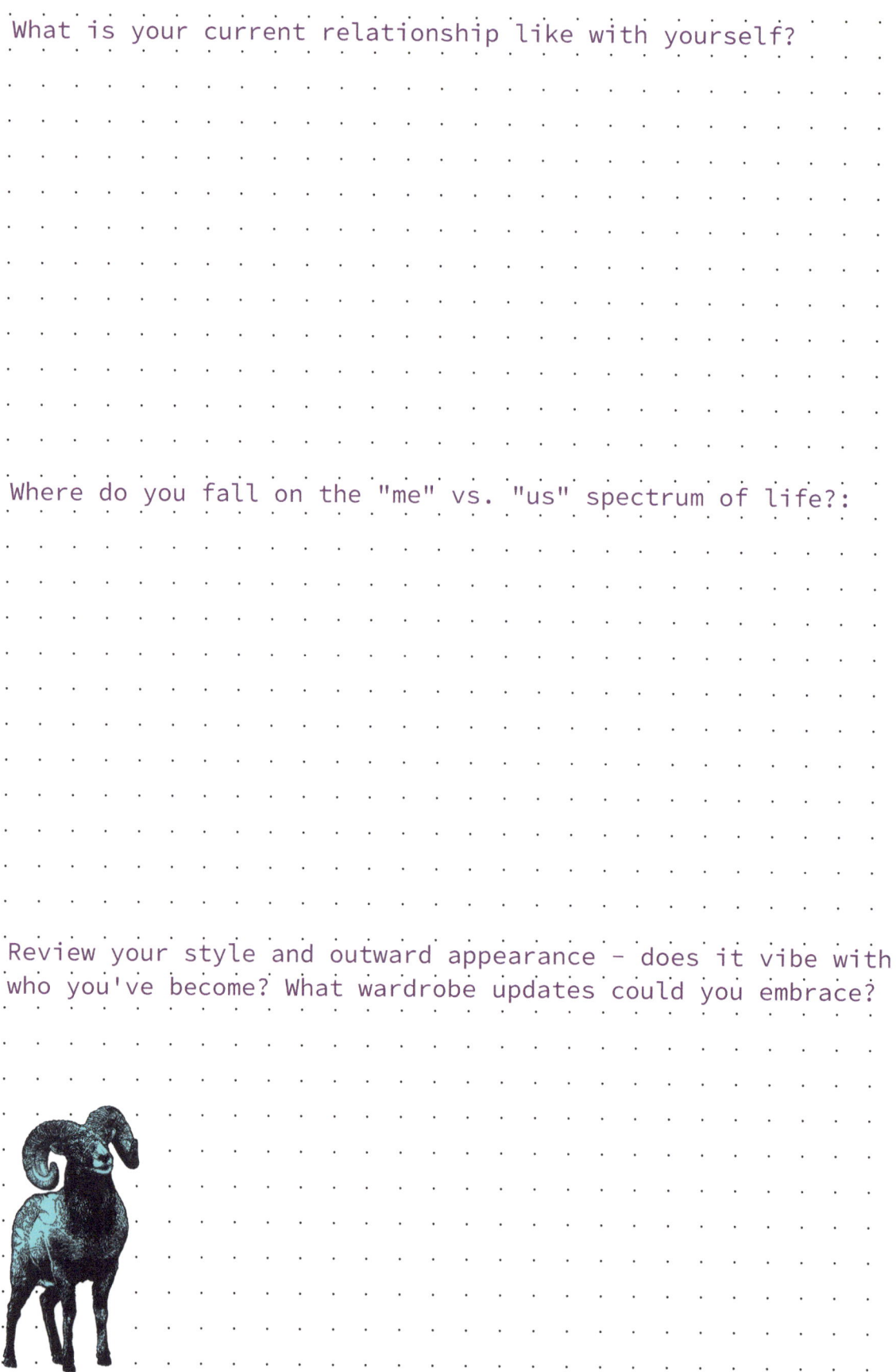

What kinds of changes would you like to see in yourself over the next year?

Write down some goals you'd like to work on this Lunar Cycle:

Write out a clear intention for this New Moon:

APR.19,'23

WEDNESDAY | WEEK 16

♈

☆

TOP TASKS:

☐
☐
☐

DAILY GRATITUDE:

6		2
7		3
8		4
9		5
10		6
11		7
12		8
1		9

NEW MOON ECLIPSE, MANIFEST (LA):

Celebrate. Consider planning
a New Moon Ritual.

MOOD:

APR.20,'23

THURSDAY | WEEK 16

♈ ♉

☆

TOP TASKS:
☐
☐
☐

DAILY GRATITUDE:

6 | 2
7 | 3
8 | 4
9 | 5
10 | 6
11 | 7
12 | 8
1 | 9

NEW MOON ECLIPSE, MANIFEST (NY, LON, SYD): Take time to set intentions + answer questions on previous page!

MOOD:

SUN → TAURUS

TOTAL SOLAR ECLIPSE!
New Moon: Manifest. Set intentions. Plant Seeds.
Follow heart. Identify goals + dreams for the new cycle.

♉

☆

TOP TASKS:

☐
☐
☐

DAILY GRATITUDE:

6	2
7	3
8	4
9	5
10	6
11	7
12	8
1	9

CRESCENT MOON, PROGRESS / WAXING:

What is 1 small action you can take today to kick off your intentions?

MOOD:

MERCURY RETROGRADE → 05.15,'23

Crescent Moon: Progress. Take Action. Trust instincts.
Make plans. Be courageous. Build good habits. Innovate.

TRACKING:

♉ ♊

TOP TASKS:
- [ ]
- [ ]
- [ ]

DAILY GRATITUDE:

6 ....

7 ....

8 ....

9 ....

10 ....

11 ....

12 ....

1 ....

2 ....

3 ....

4 ....

5 ....

6 ....

7 ....

8 ....

9 ....

CRESCENT MOON, WAXING / PROGRESS:
Which of your strengths
can help you right now?

MOOD:

TRACKING:

☆

TOP TΔSKS:
- ☐
- ☐
- ☐

DΔILY GRΔTITUDE:

6	2
7	3
8	4
9	5
10	6
11	7
12	8
1	9

CRESCENT MOON, PROGRESS / WΔXING:

What's distracting you
and how can you change it?

MOOD:

TRACKING:

♊ ♋

TOP TASKS:
- ☐
- ☐
- ☐

DAILY GRATITUDE:

6

7

8

9

10

11

12

1

2

3

4

5

6

7

8

9

CRESCENT MOON, WAXING / PROGRESS:

What kind of research can you
do to support your intentions?

MOOD:

TRACKING:

TOP TASKS:

☐

☐

☐

DAILY GRATITUDE:

6	2
7	3
8	4
9	5
10	6
11	7
12	8
1	9

CRESCENT MOON, WAXING / PROGRESS:

How can you improve
your morning routine?

MOOD:

TRACKING:

TOP TASKS:
- [ ]
- [ ]
- [ ]

DAILY GRATITUDE:

6 ....
7 ....
8 ....
9 ....
10 ....
11 ....
12 ....
1 ....

2 ....
3 ....
4 ....
5 ....
6 ....
7 ....
8 ....
9 ....

CRESCENT MOON, WAXING / PROGRESS:
How can you improve
your evening routine?

MOOD:

TRACKING:

TOP TASKS:
- [ ]
- [ ]
- [ ]

DAILY GRATITUDE:

6
7
8
9
10
11
12
1

2
3
4
5
6
7
8
9

1ST QUARTER MOON, MOTIVATE:
How are your intentions progressing
- are any adjustments necessary?

MOOD:

1st Quarter Moon: Motivate. Renew momentum.
Identify challenges. Reevaluate. Set boundaries. Adjust.

TRACKING:

TOP TASKS:
- [ ]
- [ ]
- [ ]

DAILY GRATITUDE:

6	2
7	3
8	4
9	5
10	6
11	7
12	8
1	9

GIBBOUS MOON, EXPAND / WAXING:
What can you do to
motivate yourself?

MOOD:

Gibbous Moon: Expand. Improve. Recognize luck. Connect.
Notice synchronicities. Tend to health. Listen to self

TRACKING:

♌ ♍

TOP TASKS:

☐

☐

☐

DAILY GRATITUDE:

6		2	
7		3	
8		4	
9		5	
10		6	
11		7	
12		8	
1		9	

GIBBOUS MOON, EXPAND / WAXING:

What is something
giving you hope right now?

MOOD:

TRACKING:

TOP TASKS:

☐
☐
☐

DAILY GRATITUDE:

6
7
8
9
10
11
12
1

2
3
4
5
6
7
8
9

GIBBOUS MOON, EXPAND / WAXING:
What is something
you're looking forward to?

MOOD:

♍

TRACKING:

☆

TOP TASKS:
☐
☐
☐

DAILY GRATITUDE:

6		2	
7		3	
8		4	
9		5	
10		6	
11		7	
12		8	
1		9	

GIBBOUS MOON, EXPAND / WAXING:
Where could you be
saving money or resources?

MOOD:

PLUTO RETROGRADE BEGINS → 10.11,'23

MAY 02, '23

TUESDAY | WEEK 18

♍ ♎

TRACKING:

TOP TASKS:
- [ ]
- [ ]
- [ ]

DAILY GRATITUDE:

6 ....
7 ....
8 ....
9 ....
10 ....
11 ....
12 ....
1 ....

2 ....
3 ....
4 ....
5 ....
6 ....
7 ....
8 ....
9 ....

GIBBOUS MOON, EXPAND / WAXING:

How can you be
communicating better?

MOOD:

MΔY 03, '23

♎

TRACKING:

☆

TOP TΔSKS:
- [ ]
- [ ]
- [ ]

DΔILY GRΔTITUDE:

6	2
7	3
8	4
9	5
10	6
11	7
12	8
1	9

GIBBOUS MOON, EXPΔND / WΔXING:
In what ways can you
practice self-love today?

MOOD:

TOP TASKS:
- [ ]
- [ ]
- [ ]

DAILY GRATITUDE:

6

7

8

9

10

11

12

1

2

3

4

5

6

7

8

9

GIBBOUS MOON, WAXING / EXPAND:

Who could give you
some valuable feedback?

MOOD:

SCORPIO FULL MOON ECLIPSE

"FLOWER MOON" | MAY 05, 2023

The May Full Moon is in the transformative sign of Scorpio.

A Lunar Eclipse is 3x more powerful than a regular Full Moon and is known to invite endings + demands transformations. Notably, this is the final appearance of Scorpio in the Taurus-Scorpio set (which began in Taurus 11.19.21 and ends in Taurus on 10.28.23).

Scorpio is all about passion, loyalty, devotion, persistence, death + the occult. When the Full Moon's South Node (past lives/patterns) is in Scorpio, we're asked to release + celebrate areas of death + rebirth.

Over the last ~18 months, the Taurus-Scorpio axis has challenged us to balance how we're formed vs. how we've been transformed. We've been encouraged to strive for stability, abundance + beauty in the face of death, trauma + shadow. Take time to consider your experience on these spectrums.

Opposing this Eclipse are two planets currently in Taurus: Uranus (chaos), and Mercury in Retrograde (communication mishaps). Potentially setting the stage for some edgy conversations, try to avoid controversial subjects altogether. It is also possible to receive unexpected information or inheritance.

Although endings are necessary, anything culminating now will bring monumental developments to your life.

Set the mood (page 12), then take time to respond to the Full Moon worksheet on the following pages.

Discuss any major transformations you've experienced
since Scorpio's first eclipse in the set - 05.15.22:

Which endings have relieved you the most?

Which of your vices can transform into healthier habits?:

Revisit your intentions from the last New Moon — what progress have you made? What worked, what didn't?

What are you releasing this Full Moon and why?

MAY 05, '23
FRIDAY | WEEK 18

♏

☆

TOP TASKS:
- ☐
- ☐
- ☐

DAILY GRATITUDE:

6	....	2	....
7	....	3	....
8	....	4	....
9	....	5	....
10	....	6	....
11	....	7	....
12	....	8	....
1	....	9	....

FULL MOON ECLIPSE, HARVEST (LA, NY, LON): Take time to complete the Full Moon worksheet on previous pages.

MOOD:

LUNAR ECLIPSE!
Full Moon: Enjoy. Harvest. Heal. Bloom. Have fun. Get creative. Celebrate progress. Acknowledge growth.

MAY 06,'23

♏ ↗

TRACKING:

☆

TOP TASKS:
- ☐
- ☐
- ☐

DAILY GRATITUDE:

6	2
7	3
8	4
9	5
10	6
11	7
12	8
1	9

FULL MOON ECLIPSE, HARVEST (3YD):
Take time to meditate today.

MOOD:

MAY 07, '23

○　↗

TRACKING:

☆

TOP TASKS:

☐
☐
☐

DAILY GRATITUDE:

6		2	
7		3	
8		4	
9		5	
10		6	
11		7	
12		8	
1		9	

DISSEMINATING MOON, REFLECT / WANING:

Review your boundaries — what
healthy adjustments you can make?

MOOD:

VENUS → CANCER

Disseminating Moon: Reflect. Be appreciative. Share Wisdom.
Educate. Reveal. Process. Review boundaries. Write + record.

MAY 08, '23

◑ ♐ ♑

TRACKING:

☆

TOP TASKS:
- ☐
- ☐
- ☐

DAILY GRATITUDE:

6	2
7	3
8	4
9	5
10	6
11	7
12	8
1	9

DISSEMINATING MOON, REFLECT / WANING:

Describe a recent situation
that you feel you handled well.

MOOD:

215

MAY 09,'23

TRACKING:

☆

TOP TASKS:
- [ ]
- [ ]
- [ ]

DAILY GRATITUDE:

6

7

8

9

10

11

12

1

2

3

4

5

6

7

8

9

DISSEMINATING MOON, REFLECT / WANING:
What is something you've
started that needs to be finished?

MOOD:

MAY 10, '23

♑

TRACKING:

☆

TOP TASKS:
- ☐
- ☐
- ☐

DAILY GRATITUDE:

6	2
7	3
8	4
9	5
10	6
11	7
12	8
1	9

DISSEMINATING MOON, REFLECT / WANING:
Breakdown something stopping you
which requires deeper analysis.

MOOD:

♑ ♒

TRACKING:

☆

TOP TASKS:
- [ ]
- [ ]
- [ ]

DAILY GRATITUDE:

6		2	
7		3	
8		4	
9		5	
10		6	
11		7	
12		8	
1		9	

DISSEMINATING MOON, REFLECT / WANING:
What is making you feel doubt or
fear and how can you change it?

MOOD:

MAY 12, '23
FRIDAY | WEEK 19

TRACKING:

☆

TOP TASKS:
☐
☐
☐

DAILY GRATITUDE:

6
7
8
9
10
11
12
1

2
3
4
5
6
7
8
9

LAST QUARTER MOON, RELEASE:
What can you forgive and let go of?

MOOD:

Last Quarter Moon: Release. Clear the air. Forgive.
Surrender. Embrace calm. Find balance. Clear path.

MAY 13, '23
SATURDAY | WEEK 19

≋ ♓

☆

TOP TASKS:
- ☐
- ☐
- ☐

DAILY GRATITUDE:

6		2
7		3
8		4
9		5
10		6
11		7
12		8
1		9

BALSAMIC MOON, RESTORE / WANING:
What recent wins
are you happy about?

MOOD:

Balsamic Moon: Restore. Trust intuition. Rest. Dream.
Examine ego. Find grace. Clean + declutter. Self-care.

MAY 14, '23

♓

TRACKING:

☆

TOP TASKS:

- ☐
- ☐
- ☐

DAILY GRATITUDE:

6		2
7		3
8		4
9		5
10		6
11		7
12		8
1		9

BALSAMIC MOON, RESTORE / WANING:

Is there anything
you want to quit?

MOOD:

MAY 15, '23
MONDAY | WEEK 20

♓ ♈

☆

TOP TASKS:
- ☐
- ☐
- ☐

DAILY GRATITUDE:

6		2	
7		3	
8		4	
9		5	
10		6	
11		7	
12		8	
1		9	

BALSAMIC MOON, RESTORE / WANING:
What is a piece of advice
you want to give yourself?

MOOD:

MERCURY DIRECT

MAY 16, '23

♈

TRACKING:

☆

TOP TASKS:
- [ ]
- [ ]
- [ ]

DAILY GRATITUDE:

6	2
7	3
8	4
9	5
10	6
11	7
12	8
1	9

BALSAMIC MOON, RESTORE / WANING:
What can you do to connect
deeper with your spiritual side?

MOOD:

JUPITER → TAURUS

MAY 17, '23

WEDNESDAY | WEEK 20

♈ ♉

☆

TOP TASKS:

☐
☐
☐

DAILY GRATITUDE:

6		2
7		3
8		4
9		5
10		6
11		7
12		8
1		9

BALSAMIC MOON, RESTORE / WANING:

What can you do to relax today?

MOOD:

MAY 18, '23

THURSDAY | WEEK 20

♉

TRACKING:

TOP TASKS:
- ☐
- ☐
- ☐

DAILY GRATITUDE:

6		2
7		3
8		4
9		5
10		6
11		7
12		8
1		9

BALSAMIC MOON, RESTORE / WANING:
Which habits can you continue
(or begin) this next Lunar Cycle?

MOOD:

JUPITER ⊗ PLUTO

TAURUS BLACK NEW MOON

The May New Moon occurs in the dependable sign of Taurus.

Also known as a Black Moon, this is the 3rd New Moon in a Season of 4 New Moons. 2023 has been packed with powerful New Moons and this one is just as big - perfect for getting in touch with your best intentions, and adjusting both long-term and short-term goals.

Taurus is all about abundance, stability, hard work, honesty, comfort, ambition, and luxury. This New Moon encourages us to enjoy simple pleasures, revel in beauty + connect with our feminine side.

Mars/Cancer (action) and Neptune/Pisces (fantasy), combine efforts to supercharge this New Moon by supporting new money-making endeavors. Passion projects are poised to turn profitable. It's time for creative expressions + making dreams a reality.

Although the Moon forms a positive Aspect with Pluto/Aquarius (power), she will also form a hard angle to Saturn/Pisces (discipline). Because Mars is working in our favor, beware of this match-up turning a good thing bad: passion can invite tensions, excitement may turn anxious + tenacity may be deemed extreme.

An auspicious Black New Moon such as this reminds us to consider our relationship with abundance + appreciate our dearest possessions. Find gratitude for whatever brings you security. Anytime the Moon is in Taurus is a chance to feel beautiful + indulge our most luxurious desires.

Set the mood (page 12), then take time to respond to the New Moon worksheet on the following pages.

Describe a passion project which has a potential for profit:

What is the significance behind your favorite possession?

Describe your current relationship with money:

What makes you feel beautiful?

Write down some goals you'd like to work on this Lunar Cycle:

Write out a clear intention for this New Moon:

MAY 19, '23

FRIDAY | WEEK 20

♉ ♊

TRACKING:

☆

TOP TASKS:

☐

☐

☐

DAILY GRATITUDE:

6		2	
7		3	
8		4	
9		5	
10		6	
11		7	
12		8	
1		9	

NEW "BLACK" MOON, MANIFEST (LA, NY, LON): Take time to complete the New Moon worksheet on previous pages.

MOOD:

New Moon: Manifest. Set intentions. Plant Seeds. Follow heart. Identify goals + dreams for the new cycle.

MAY 20, '23

♊

TRACKING:

☆

TOP TASKS:
- ☐
- ☐
- ☐

DAILY GRATITUDE:

6		2	
7		3	
8		4	
9		5	
10		6	
11		7	
12		8	
1		9	

NEW "BLACK" MOON, MANIFEST (SYD):
Meditate on new
or revived intentions.

MOOD:

MARS → LEO

MAY 21, '23

SUNDAY | WEEK 20

♊

TRACKING:

☆

TOP TASKS:
- ☐
- ☐
- ☐

DAILY GRATITUDE:

6	2
7	3
8	4
9	5
10	6
11	7
12	8
1	9

CRESCENT MOON, PROGRESS / WAXING:

What is 1 small action you can take today to kick off your intentions?

MOOD:

SUN → GEMINI

Crescent Moon: Progress. Take Action. Trust instincts.
Make plans. Be courageous. Build good habits. Innovate.

MAY 22, '23

♊ ♋

TRACKING:

☆

TOP TASKS:

☐
☐
☐

DAILY GRATITUDE:

6	2
7	3
8	4
9	5
10	6
11	7
12	8
1	9

CRESCENT MOON, PROGRESS / WAXING:

Which of your strengths
can help you now?

MOOD:

TRACKING:

☆

TOP TASKS:

☐
☐
☐

DAILY GRATITUDE:

6	2
7	3
8	4
9	5
10	6
11	7
12	8
1	9

CRESCENT MOON, WAXING / PROGRESS:
What's distracting you
and how can you change it?

MOOD:

MAY 24, '23

WEDNESDAY | WEEK 21

♋ ♌

☆

TOP TASKS:

- [ ]
- [ ]
- [ ]

DAILY GRATITUDE:

6

7

8

9

10

11

12

1

2

3

4

5

6

7

8

9

CRESCENT MOON, WAXING / PROGRESS:

What kind of research can
you do to support your intentions?

MOOD:

MAY 25, '23

♌

TRACKING:

☆

TOP TASKS:
- [ ]
- [ ]
- [ ]

DAILY GRATITUDE:

6 ....

7 ....

8 ....

9 ....

10 ....

11 ....

12 ....

1 ....

2 ....

3 ....

4 ....

5 ....

6 ....

7 ....

8 ....

9 ....

CRESCENT MOON, WAXING / PROGRESS:
How can you improve
your morning routine?

MOOD:

MAY 26, '23
FRIDAY | WEEK 21

♌

☆

TOP TASKS:
- ☐
- ☐
- ☐

DAILY GRATITUDE:

6

7

8

9

10

11

12

1

2

3

4

5

6

7

8

9

CRESCENT MOON, WAXING / PROGRESS:

How can you improve
your evening routine?

MOOD:

MAY 27, '23
SATURDAY | WEEK 21

☽ ♌ ♍

TRACKING:

☆

TOP TASKS:
☐
☐
☐

DAILY GRATITUDE:

6		2	
7		3	
8		4	
9		5	
10		6	
11		7	
12		8	
1		9	

1ST QUARTER MOON, MOTIVATE:
How are your intentions progressing - do you need adjustments?

MOOD:

1st Quarter Moon: Motivate. Renew momentum. Identify challenges. Reevaluate. Set boundaries. Adjust.

MAY 28, '23

SUNDAY | WEEK 21

♍

☆

TOP TASKS:

☐
☐
☐

DAILY GRATITUDE:

6	2
7	3
8	4
9	5
10	6
11	7
12	8
1	9

GIBBOUS MOON, EXPAND / WAXING:

What can you do
to motivate yourself?

MOOD:

Gibbous Moon: Expand. Improve. Recognize luck. Connect.
Notice synchronicities. Tend to health. Listen to self.

MAY 29, '23
MONDAY | WEEK 22

♏ ♎

TRACKING:

☆

TOP TASKS:
- ☐
- ☐
- ☐

DAILY GRATITUDE:

6		2	
7		3	
8		4	
9		5	
10		6	
11		7	
12		8	
1		9	

GIBBOUS MOON, EXPAND / WAXING:
What is something
giving you hope right now?

MOOD:

MAY 30, '23
TUESDAY | WEEK 22

☽ ♎ ☆

TOP TASKS:
- [ ]
- [ ]
- [ ]

DAILY GRATITUDE:

6 ....

7 ....

8 ....

9 ....

10 ....

11 ....

12 ....

1 ....

2 ....

3 ....

4 ....

5 ....

6 ....

7 ....

8 ....

9 ....

GIBBOUS MOON, EXPAND / WAXING:
What is something you
are looking forward to?

MOOD:

MAY 31, '23

WEDNESDAY | WEEK 22

☽ ♎ ♏

TRACKING:

☆

TOP TASKS:
- ☐
- ☐
- ☐

DAILY GRATITUDE:

6		2	
7		3	
8		4	
9		5	
10		6	
11		7	
12		8	
1		9	

GIBBOUS MOON, EXPAND / WAXING:
Where could you be
saving money or resources?

MOOD:

☾   ♏

TRACKING:

☆

TOP TASKS:
- ☐
- ☐
- ☐

DAILY GRATITUDE:

6	2
7	3
8	4
9	5
10	6
11	7
12	8
1	9

GIBBOUS MOON, EXPAND / WAXING:
How can you be communicating better?

MOOD:

JUN.02,'23

♏

TRACKING:

☆

TOP TASKS:
☐
☐
☐

DAILY GRATITUDE:

6 ....
7 ....
8 ....
9 ....
10 ....
11 ....
12 ....
1 ....

2 ....
3 ....
4 ....
5 ....
6 ....
7 ....
8 ....
9 ....

GIBBOUS MOON, EXPAND / WAXING:
Who could give you
some valuable feedback?

MOOD:

SAGITTARIUS FULL MOON

"STRAWBERRY MOON" | JUNE 04, 2023

The June Full Moon is in the carefree sign of Sagittarius. Depending on your time zone this Moon may appear on 06.03.

Sagittarius is all about adventure, philosophy, adaptability, travel, humor, optimism + the quest for knowledge. This Full Moon serves as a reminder that there is always more to experience + learn.

Opposite the Full Moon is the Sun in Gemini, which is social, chatty, playful + curious. Therefore, the Gemini-Sagittarius Sun-Moon polarity challenges us to balance street smarts vs. book smarts. To travel local vs. travel global. Take time to evaluate where you fall on this spectrum.

Highlighting our desire to find meaning, this Full Moon invites us to embrace our wanderlust. Cooped up for too long, the pandemic restrained our ability to travel freely. Reinvigorated to tick off our bucket lists and see the world, we're motivated to roam - whether it's globe-trotting foreign countries or strolling through local museums.

The Moon is squaring Neptune/Pisces (fantasy) causing both confusion + determination. After collectively spending ~3 years in a state of uncertainty, we may experience levels of hypersensitivity + nervousness around the very idea of travel. Take whatever precautions you feel necessary and give respect to others who choose to navigate this world differently than you do. Over in the sign of Taurus, Uranus (chaos) is vibing with Mercury (communication), welcoming a positive environment for unique ideas + points of view.

Set the mood (page 12), then take time to respond to the Full Moon worksheet on the following pages.

If you could travel anywhere, where it would be and why?
Think local + global:

Describe something that you'd like to learn:

How are you street smart vs. book smart?

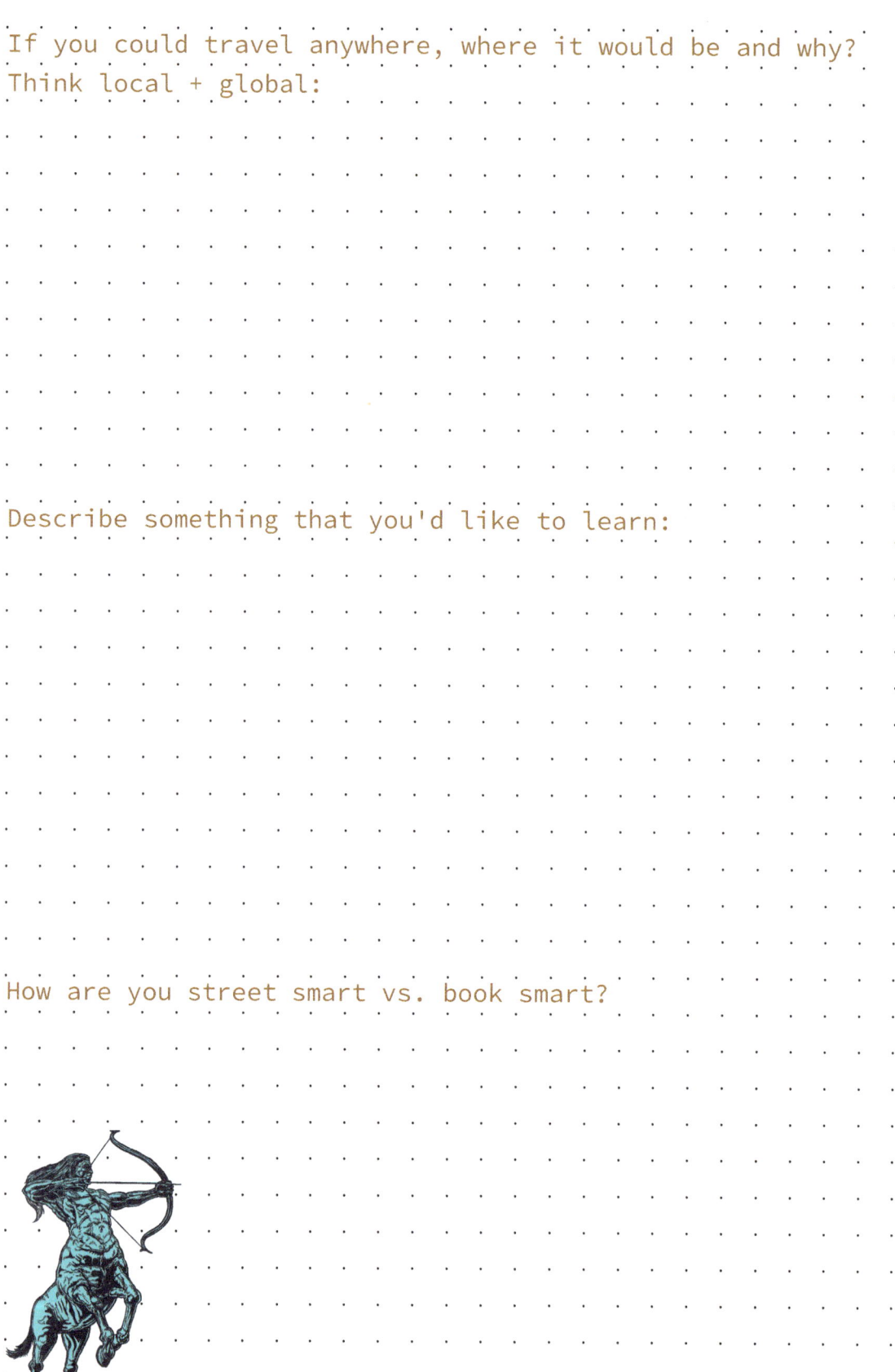

List 10 things on your bucket list:

Revisit your intentions from the last New Moon — what progress have you made? What worked, what didn't?

What are you releasing this Full Moon and why?

♏ ↗

TRACKING:

☆

TOP TASKS:
- [ ]
- [ ]
- [ ]

DAILY GRATITUDE:

6

2

7

3

8

4

9

5

10

6

11

7

12

8

1

9

FULL MOON, HARVEST (LA):
Take time to celebrate yourself!

MOOD:

⌖

☆

TOP TASKS:
- ☐
- ☐
- ☐

DAILY GRATITUDE:

6	2
7	3
8	4
9	5
10	6
11	7
12	8
1	9

FULL MOON, HARVEST (NY, LON, SYD):
Set intentions + complete Full Moon
worksheet on the previous pages.

MOOD:

Full Moon: Enjoy. Harvest. Heal. Bloom. Have fun.
Get creative. Celebrate progress. Acknowledge growth.

JUN.05,'23

○   ↗ ♑

TRACKING:

☆

TOP TASKS:
- ☐
- ☐
- ☐

DAILY GRATITUDE:

6	2
7	3
8	4
9	5
10	6
11	7
12	8
1	9

DISSEMINATING MOON, REFLECT / WANING:
Describe a recent situation
that you feel you handled well.

MOOD:

VENUS → LEO

Disseminating Moon: Reflect. Be appreciative. Share Wisdom.
Educate. Reveal. Process. Review boundaries. Write + record.

♑

☆

TOP TASKS:
- ☐
- ☐
- ☐

DAILY GRATITUDE:

6		2
7		3
8		4
9		5
10		6
11		7
12		8
1		9

DISSEMINATING MOON, REFLECT / WANING:

What is something you've
started that needs to be finished?

MOOD:

TRACKING:

☆

TOP TASKS:

☐

☐

☐

DAILY GRATITUDE:

6		2	
7		3	
8		4	
9		5	
10		6	
11		7	
12		8	
1		9	

DISSEMINATING MOON, REFLECT / WANING:

Breakdown something stopping you
which requires deeper analysis.

MOOD:

JUN.08,'23

TRACKING:

TOP TASKS:
- [ ]
- [ ]
- [ ]

DAILY GRATITUDE:

6	2
7	3
8	4
9	5
10	6
11	7
12	8
1	9

DISSEMINATING MOON, REFLECT / WANING:
How can you share what
you've learned with others?

MOOD:

TRACKING:

☆

TOP TASKS:
☐
☐
☐

DAILY GRATITUDE:

6		2	
7		3	
8		4	
9		5	
10		6	
11		7	
12		8	
1		9	

DISSEMINATING MOON, REFLECT / WANING:

Review your boundaries - what
healthy adjustments can you make?

MOOD:

♓

TRACKING:

☆

TOP TASKS:
- ☐
- ☐
- ☐

DAILY GRATITUDE:

6 ....

7 ....

8 ....

9 ....

10 ....

11 ....

12 ....

1 ....

2 ....

3 ....

4 ....

5 ....

6 ....

7 ....

8 ....

9 ....

LAST QUARTER MOON, RELEASE:
What can you forgive + let go of?

MOOD:

Last Quarter Moon: Release. Clear the air. Forgive.
Surrender. Embrace calm. Find balance. Clear path.

♓ ♈

TRACKING:

☆

TOP TASKS:

☐

☐

☐

DAILY GRATITUDE:

6 ....

7 ....

8 ....

9 ....

10 ....

11 ....

12 ....

1 ....

2 ....

3 ....

4 ....

5 ....

6 ....

7 ....

8 ....

9 ....

BALSAMIC MOON, RESTORE / WANING:

What recent wins
are you happy about?

MOOD:

PLUTO → CAPRICORN
MERCURY → GEMINI

Balsamic Moon: Restore. Trust intuition. Rest. Dream.
Examine ego. Find grace. Clean + declutter. Self-care.

♈

☆

TOP TASKS:
- [ ]
- [ ]
- [ ]

DAILY GRATITUDE:

6
7
8
9
10
11
12
1

2
3
4
5
6
7
8
9

BALSAMIC MOON, RESTORE / WANING:
Is there anything
you want to quit?

MOOD:

♈ ♉

☆

TOP TASKS:

☐

☐

☐

DAILY GRATITUDE:

6

7

8

9

10

11

12

1

2

3

4

5

6

7

8

9

BALSAMIC MOON, RESTORE / WANING:

What is a piece of advice
you want to give yourself?

MOOD:

JUN.14,'23

♉

TRACKING:

☆

TOP TASKS:
- ☐
- ☐
- ☐

DAILY GRATITUDE:

6	2
7	3
8	4
9	5
10	6
11	7
12	8
1	9

BALSAMIC MOON, RESTORE / WANING:
What can you do to connect deeper with your spiritual side?

MOOD:

TRACKING:

☆

TOP TASKS:
☐
☐
☐

DAILY GRATITUDE:

6	2
7	3
8	4
9	5
10	6
11	7
12	8
1	9

BALSAMIC MOON, RESTORE / WANING:
What can you do to relax today?

MOOD:

JUN.16,'23
FRIDAY | WEEK 24

♈ ♊

☆

TOP TASKS:
- ☐
- ☐
- ☐

DAILY GRATITUDE:

6		2	
7		3	
8		4	
9		5	
10		6	
11		7	
12		8	
1		9	

BALSAMIC MOON, RESTORE / WANING:
Which habits can you continue
(or begin) this next Lunar Cycle?

MOOD:

GEMINI NEW MOON

JUNE 18, 2023

The June New Moon is in the social sign of Gemini.
Depending on your time zone this Moon may occur on 06.17.

Gemini is all about communication, charisma, quick-wit,
responsiveness + persuasion. This New Moon encourages us
to express ourselves - ideally with friends.

Neptune (fantasy), in it's home sign of Pisces, is forming
a square with the Sun and throwing up all sorts of red flags.
We are reminded to keep our insecurities at bay, for
overcompensation may only increase anxieties.

Saturn/Pisces (discipline), stations Retrograde this week
for the next ~4 months. We're asked to take responsibility
for self-regulation by replacing addictive + distractive
impulses with positive activity, like exercising, reading
or listing to music. Consider quitting whatever has been
unhealthy for you. Beware of escapism, overindulgence +
delusions of grandeur. We are encouraged to rely on our
sense spirit + spirituality when dealing with overwhelming
or irrational fears.

A Gemini New Moon inspires us to be social. Take time to
identify who you'd like to spend time with + what activities
you want to do together. Whether it's one-on-one, or with a
larger group of trustworthy friends, find ways to have a good
time. As much as possible, disengage from any form of
negative self-talk, gossip, or other two-faced behaviors -
it's beneath us, anyway.

Set the mood (page 12), then take time to respond
to the New Moon worksheet on the following pages.

Describe your ideal social activity - who is there?

What is currently causing you confusion or self-doubt?

How can you be communicating better?

List your favorite books, poems, songs and speeches:

Write down some goals you'd like to work on this Lunar Cycle:

Write out a clear intention for this New Moon:

♊

☆

TOP TASKS:
- [ ]
- [ ]
- [ ]

DAILY GRATITUDE:

6	2
7	3
8	4
9	5
10	6
11	7
12	8
1	9

NEW MOON, MANIFEST (LA):

Consider your intentions and make space for a New Moon Ritual.

MOOD:

SATURN RETROGRADE BEGINS → 11.04,'23

JUN.18,'23

SUNDAY | WEEK 24

♊ ♋

☆

TOP TASKS:

- ☐
- ☐
- ☐

DAILY GRATITUDE:

6

7

8

9

10

11

12

1

2

3

4

5

6

7

8

9

NEW MOON, MANIFEST (NY, LON, SYD):

Take time to complete the New Moon
worksheet on the previous pages.

MOOD:

New Moon: Manifest. Set intentions. Plant Seeds.
Follow heart. Identify goals + dreams for the new cycle.

JUN.19,'23
MONDAY | WEEK 25

♋

☆

TOP TASKS:
☐
☐
☐

DAILY GRATITUDE:

6		2
7		3
8		4
9		5
10		6
11		7
12		8
1		9

CRESCENT MOON, PROGRESS / WAXING:
What is 1 small action you can take today to kick off your intentions?

MOOD:

JUPITER ♥ SATURN

Crescent Moon: Progress. Take Action. Trust instincts.
Make plans. Be courageous. Build good habits. Innovate.

♋ ♌

TRACKING:

TOP TASKS:
- [ ]
- [ ]
- [ ]

DAILY GRATITUDE:

6

7

8

9

10

11

12

1

2

3

4

5

6

7

8

9

CRESCENT MOON, PROGRESS / WAXING:

Which of your strengths
can help you now?

MOOD:

♌

TRACKING:

☆

TOP TASKS:
- [ ]
- [ ]
- [ ]

DAILY GRATITUDE:

6		2	
7		3	
8		4	
9		5	
10		6	
11		7	
12		8	
1		9	

CRESCENT MOON, PROGRESS / WAXING:
What's distracting you
and how can you change it?

MOOD:

SUN → CANCER

N. HEMISPHERE - SUMMER SOLSTICE
S. HEMISPHERE - WINTER SOLSTICE

JUN.22,'23

THURSDAY | WEEK 25

♌

☆

TOP TASKS:

- [ ]
- [ ]
- [ ]

DAILY GRATITUDE:

6		2	
7		3	
8		4	
9		5	
10		6	
11		7	
12		8	
1		9	

CRESCENT MOON, WAXING / PROGRESS:

What kind of research can you
do to support your intentions?

MOOD:

♌ ♍

TRACKING:

TOP TASKS:
- [ ]
- [ ]
- [ ]

DAILY GRATITUDE:

6	2
7	3
8	4
9	5
10	6
11	7
12	8
1	9

CRESCENT MOON, WAXING / PROGRESS:

How can you improve
your morning routine?

MOOD:

♍

TRACKING:

☆

TOP TASKS:
- [ ]
- [ ]
- [ ]

DAILY GRATITUDE:

6	2
7	3
8	4
9	5
10	6
11	7
12	8
1	9

CRESCENT MOON, PROGRESS / WAXING:

How can you improve
your evening routine?

MOOD:

♍ ♎

TRACKING:

☆

TOP TASKS:

☐
☐
☐

DAILY GRATITUDE:

6
7
8
9
10
11
12
1

2
3
4
5
6
7
8
9

CRESCENT MOON, WAXING / PROGRESS:
Describe a moment of progress
you had this week -big or small.

MOOD:

♎︎

TRACKING:

☆

TOP TASKS:

☐
☐
☐

DAILY GRATITUDE:

6		2
7		3
8		4
9		5
10		6
11		7
12		8
1		9

1ST QUARTER MOON, MOTIVATE:

How are your intentions progressing - do you need to make adjustments?

MOOD:

MERCURY → CANCER

1st Quarter Moon: Motivate. Renew momentum. Identify challenges. Reevaluate. Set boundaries. Adjust.

♎

TRACKING:

☆

TOP TASKS:
- ☐
- ☐
- ☐

DAILY GRATITUDE:

6	2
7	3
8	4
9	5
10	6
11	7
12	8
1	9

GIBBOUS MOON, EXPAND / WAXING:
What is something you're
looking forward to?

MOOD:

Gibbous Moon: Expand. Improve. Recognize luck. Connect.
Notice synchronicities. Tend to health. Listen to self.

TRACKING:

TOP TASKS:

☐
☐
☐

DAILY GRATITUDE:

6
7
8
9
10
11
12
1

2
3
4
5
6
7
8
9

GIBBOUS MOON, WAXING / EXPAND:
Where could you be
saving money or resources?

MOOD:

♏

TRACKING:

☆

TOP TASKS:
☐
☐
☐

DAILY GRATITUDE:

6	2
7	3
8	4
9	5
10	6
11	7
12	8
1	9

GIBBOUS MOON, WAXING / EXPAND:
How could you be
communicating better?

MOOD:

♏ ♐

TRACKING:

☆

TOP T∆SKS:
- [ ]
- [ ]
- [ ]

DAILY GR∆TITUDE:

6

7

8

9

10

11

12

1

2

3

4

5

6

7

8

9

GIBBOUS MOON, W∆XING / EXP∆ND:
In what ways can you
practice self-love today?

MOOD:

NEPTUNE RETROGR∆DE BEGINS → 12.06,'23

STATE-OF-SELF 6-MONTH CHECK-IN

Revisit page 20 + 164 to compare, track + acknowledge your growth. Based on the Astrological Houses, rate each area of life 1-10 and make notes in the space provided. Identify areas which deserve attention, improvement + appreciation.

How do I feel about myself?   1 2 3 4 5 6 7 8 9 10
- -
- -
- -

How stable is my life?   1 2 3 4 5 6 7 8 9 10
- -
- -
- -

How is my communication?   1 2 3 4 5 6 7 8 9 10
- -
- -
- -

How is my home life?   1 2 3 4 5 6 7 8 9 10
- -
- -
- -

How much am I enjoying myself?   1 2 3 4 5 6 7 8 9 10
- -
- -
- -

How is my physical health?   1 2 3 4 5 6 7 8 9 10
- -
- -
- -

How are my relationships?   1 2 3 4 5 6 7 8 9 10

How am I coping with change?   1 2 3 4 5 6 7 8 9 10

How much am I learning?   1 2 3 4 5 6 7 8 9 10

How is my reputation / career?   1 2 3 4 5 6 7 8 9 10

How are my friendships / community?   1 2 3 4 5 6 7 8 9 10

How is my sleep / self-care?   1 2 3 4 5 6 7 8 9 10

Areas of Attention and Appreciation Over Next 3 Months:

INDEX OF PLANETARY EVENTS

JANUARY

- 01.03 ▷ Venus → Aquarius
- 01.06 ○ Full Moon, Cancer
- 01.12 → Mars Direct → Gemini
- 01.15 | Last Quarter Moon, Libra
- 01.18 → Mercury Direct → Capricorn
- 01.20 ☼ Sun → Aquarius
- 01.21 ● Super New Moon, Aquarius
- 01.22 → Uranus Direct → Taurus
- 01.27 ▷ Venus → Pisces
- 01.28 | 1st Quarter Moon, Taurus

FEBRUARY

- 02.05 ○ Full Moon, Leo
- 02.11 ▷ Mercury → Aquarius
- 02.13 | Last Quarter Moon, Scorpio
- 02.18 ☼ Sun → Pisces
- 02.20 ● Super New Moon, Pisces
- 02.20 ▷ Venus → Aries
- 02.27 | 1st Quarter Moon, Gemini

MARCH

- 03.02 ▷ Mercury → Pisces
- 03.07 ○ Full Moon, Virgo
- 03.07 ▷ Saturn → Pisces
- 03.12 ✳ Jupiter ♥ Chiron
- 03.15 | Last Quarter Moon, Sagittarius
- 03.16 ▷ Venus → Taurus
- 03.19 ▷ Mercury → Aries
- 03.20 ☼ Sun → Aries
- 03.20 △ Spring Equinox
- 03.21 ● New Moon, Aries
- 03.23 ▷ Pluto → Aquarius
- 03.25 ▷ Mars → Cancer
- 03.29 | 1st Quarter Moon, Cancer

APRIL

- 04.03 ▷ Mercury → Taurus
- 04.06 ○ Full Moon, Libra
- 04.11 ▷ Venus → Gemini
- 04.13 | Last Quarter Moon, Capricorn
- 04.20 • New Moon Total Solar Eclipse, Aries (Aries-Libra set)
- 04.20 ☼ Sun → Taurus
- 04.21 ← Mercury Retrograde ← Taurus (05.15)
- 04.27 | 1st Quarter Moon, Leo

MAY

- 05.01 ← Pluto Retrograde ← Aquarius (10.11)
- 05.05 ☾ Full Moon Lunar Eclipse, Scorpio (Taurus-Scorpio set)
- 05.07 ▷ Venus → Cancer
- 05.12 | Last Quarter Moon, Aquarius
- 05.15 → Mercury Direct → Taurus
- 05.16 ▷ Jupiter → Taurus
- 05.18 ✳ Jupiter ⊗ Pluto
- 05.19 • Black New Moon, Taurus
- 05.20 ▷ Mars → Leo
- 05.21 ☼ Sun → Gemini
- 05.27 | 1st Quarter Moon, Virgo

JUNE

- 06.04 ○ Full Moon, Sagittarius
- 06.05 ▷ Venus → Leo
- 06.10 | Last Quarter Moon, Pisces
- 06.11 ← Pluto (mid-Retrograde) ← Capricorn
- 06.11 ▷ Mercury → Gemini
- 06.17 ← Saturn Retrograde ← Pisces (11.04)
- 06.18 • New Moon, Gemini
- 06.19 ✳ Jupiter ♥ Saturn
- 06.21 ☼ Sun → Cancer
- 06.21 △ Summer Solstice
- 06.26 | 1st Quarter Moon, Libra
- 06.26 ▷ Mercury → Cancer
- 06.30 ← Neptune Retrograde ← Pisces (12.06)

JULY

- 07.03 ○ Full Moon, Capricorn
- 07.10 | Last Quarter Moon, Aries
- 07.10 ▷ Mars → Virgo
- 07.11 ▷ Mercury → Leo
- 07.17 ● New Moon, Cancer
- 07.23 ← Venus Retrograde ← Leo (09.04)
- 07.23 ☼ Sun → Leo
- 07.23 ← Chiron Retrograde ← Aries (12.27)
- 07.25 | 1st Quarter Moon, Libra
- 07.28 ▷ Mercury → Virgo

AUGUST

- 08.01 ○ Super Full Moon, Aquarius
- 08.08 | Last Quarter Moon, Taurus
- 08.16 ● New Moon, Leo
- 08.23 ☼ Sun → Virgo
- 08.23 ← Mercury Retrograde ← Virgo (09.15)
- 08.24 | 1st Quarter Moon, Sagittarius
- 08.27 ▷ Mars → Libra
- 08.29 ← Uranus Retrograde ← Taurus (01.27.24)
- 08.31 ○ Super Full Blue Moon, Pisces

SEPTEMBER

- 09.04 → Venus Direct → Leo
- 09.04 ← Jupiter Retrograde ← Taurus (12.30)
- 09.06 | Last Quarter Moon, Gemini
- 09.15 ● New Moon, Virgo
- 09.15 → Mercury Direct → Virgo
- 09.22 | 1st Quarter Moon, Sagittarius
- 09.23 ☼ Sun → Libra
- 09.23 △ Fall Equinox
- 09.29 ○ Full Moon, Aries

OCTOBER

- 10.05 ▷ Mercury → Libra
- 10.07 | Last Quarter Moon, Cancer
- 10.09 ▷ Venus → Virgo
- 10.11 → Pluto Direct → Capricorn
- 10.12 ▷ Mars → Scorpio
- 10.14 ☾ New Moon Annular Solar Eclipse, Libra (Aries-Libra set)
- 10.22 | 1st Quarter Moon, Capricorn
- 10.22 ▷ Mercury → Scorpio
- 10.23 ☼ Sun → Scorpio
- 10.28 ☾ Full Moon Lunar Eclipse, Taurus (Taurus-Scorpio set)

NOVEMBER

- 11.04 → Saturn Direct → Pisces
- 11.05 | Last Quarter Moon, Leo
- 11.08 ▷ Venus → Libra
- 11.10 ▷ Mercury → Sagittarius
- 11.13 ● New Moon, Scorpio
- 11.20 | 1st Quarter Moon, Aquarius
- 11.22 ☼ Sun → Sagittarius
- 11.24 ▷ Mars → Sagittarius
- 11.27 ○ Full Moon, Gemini

DECEMBER

- 12.01 ▷ Mercury → Capricorn
- 12.04 ▷ Venus → Scorpio
- 12.05 | Last Quarter Moon, Virgo
- 12.06 → Neptune Direct → Pisces
- 12.12 ● New Moon, Sagittarius
- 12.13 ← Mercury Retrograde Capricorn (01.01.24)
- 12.19 | 1st Quarter Moon, Pisces
- 12.22 ☼ Sun → Capricorn
- 12.22 △ Winter Solstice
- 12.23 ← Mercury (mid-Retrograde) ← Sagittarius
- 12.26 ○ Full Moon, Cancer
- 12.27 → Chiron Direct → Aries
- 12.29 ▷ Venus → Sagittarius
- 12.30 → Jupiter Direct → Taurus

TO ORDER ANOTHER MOON TIME PLANNER,

OR ANY OF THE ART FEATURED,

PLEASE VISIT OUR WEBSITE:

WWW.MOONTIMEPLANNER.COM

www.ingramcontent.com/pod-product-compliance
Lightning Source LLC
Chambersburg PA
CBHW041508120626
46551CB00018B/2352